GIRLS
BEHAVING
~~BADLY~~
WORSE

EDITED BY
NICHOLA HEGARTY

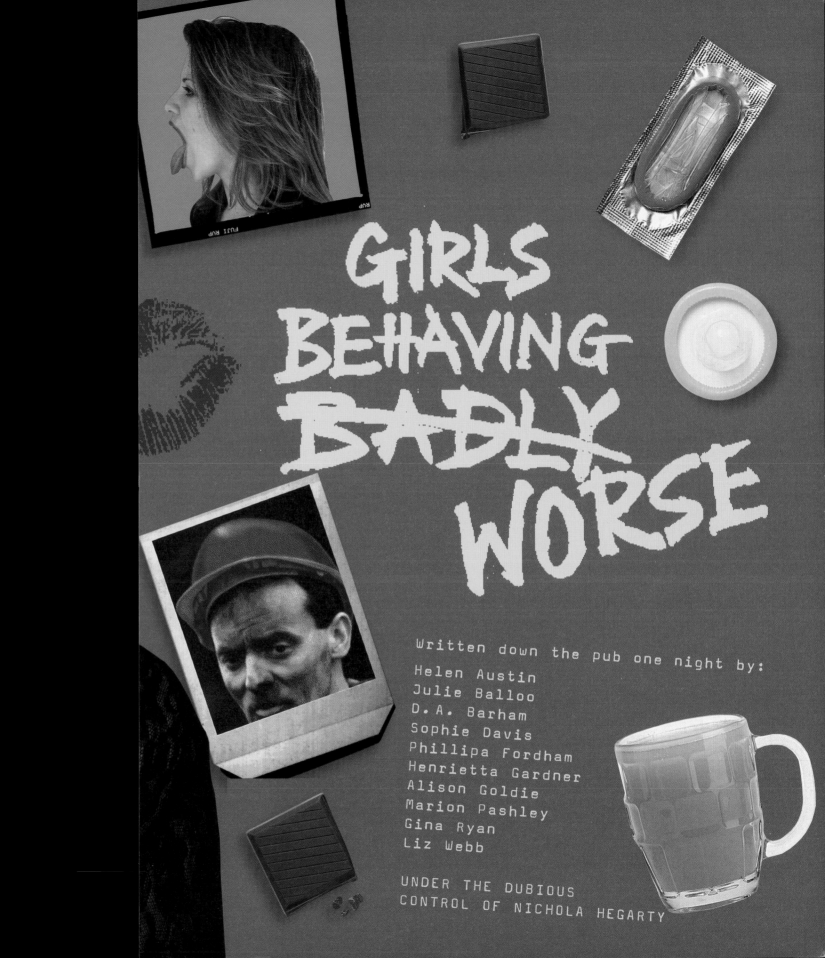

GIRLS BEHAVING ~~BADLY~~ WORSE

Written down the pub one night by:

Helen Austin
Julie Balloo
D.A. Barham
Sophie Davis
Phillipa Fordham
Henrietta Gardner
Alison Goldie
Marion Pashley
Gina Ryan
Liz Webb

UNDER THE DUBIOUS
CONTROL OF NICHOLA HEGARTY

The other night...

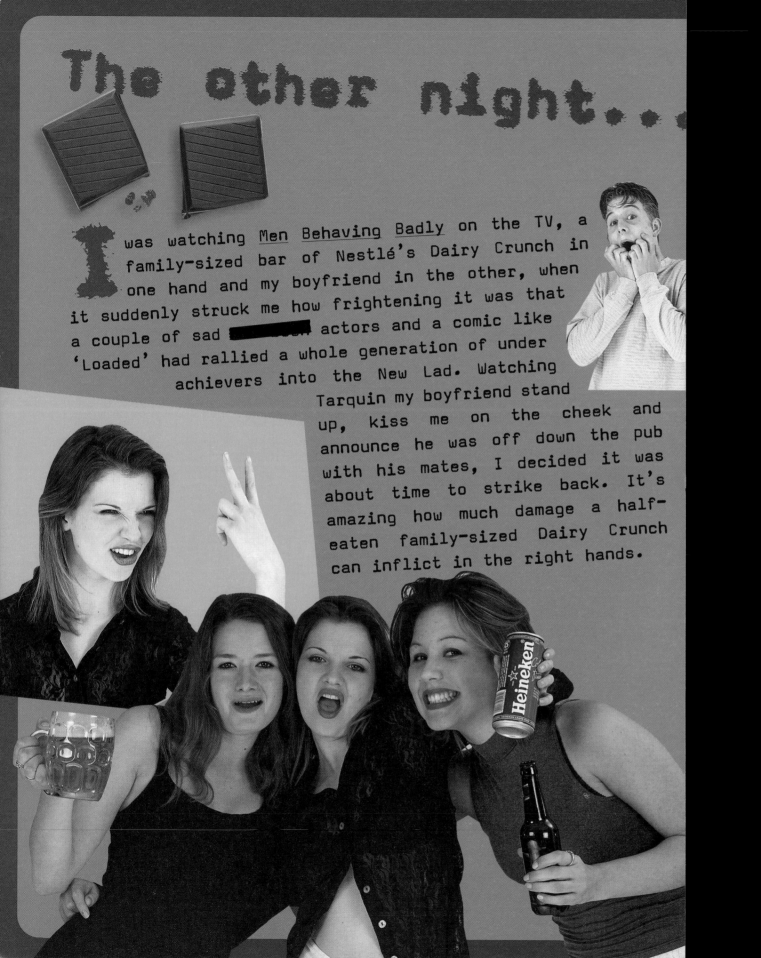

I was watching <u>Men</u> <u>Behaving</u> <u>Badly</u> on the TV, a family-sized bar of Nestlé's Dairy Crunch in one hand and my boyfriend in the other, when it suddenly struck me how frightening it was that a couple of sad ██████ actors and a comic like 'Loaded' had rallied a whole generation of under achievers into the New Lad. Watching Tarquin my boyfriend stand up, kiss me on the cheek and announce he was off down the pub with his mates, I decided it was about time to strike back. It's amazing how much damage a half-eaten family-sized Dairy Crunch can inflict in the right hands.

He was soon out of the door followed by his Euro '96 sticker collection, poster of Danii Minogue, a sad sculpture of a naked woman made from 16,482 Stella ring Pulls and his six videos of $9\frac{1}{2}$ weeks.

Let's face it

it's time to take back our bodies and wear them... or something like that. So me and the girls stopped shopping for a couple of days, forgot the hip and thigh diet, ripped down the distracting posters of Patrick Swayze, Richard E. Grant and John Major in jockey shorts and penned this little treasure trove of advice. Sadly we had to rely on our own literary talents as Sharon Stone, Carol Vorderman, Zoe Ball and Yasmin Le Bon couldn't come round and help... but then we didn't ask them, so what can you expect.

RULES OF THE

VISITORS BY PRIOR APPOINTMENT ONLY

You don't want any Tom, Dick or Harry popping round when you're singing Madonna songs on your "Home Karaoke" wearing nothing but some big grey pants and a pair of slipper socks.

NO JEHOVAH'S WITNESSES OR REPRESENTATIVES FROM ANY NUTTY MOVEMENT

If you've been on your own for three days, you sometimes get lonely, invite callers in and then you're stuck with them droning on for hours… (and what if they hypnotise and kidnap you, and you become a zombie, Bible-spouting loser like them …AAAAArgh!)

IF YOU WANT TO EAT, BRING YOUR OWN

Single girls who do not have to cater for anyone else tend to indulge in eccentric foodstuffs which may not be to your taste. A typical single girl's cupboard contains: bag of nut-burger mix, dried seaweed, weird-shaped pasta and rice with bits in, packet of 5-day weight-loss-programme sachets, Bombay mix, six-pack of American muffins, Jammy Dodgers, celeriac, yams, vitamin pills.

ALL LIVING THINGS TO BE RESPECTED

In lieu of flatmates or a partner, the single girl collects cats, the odd reptile, a lot of pot plants and strange sprouting things in jars. She gives them maternal nurture and they are her confidantes, patiently listening to her tales of emotional devastation. Sometimes it seems as though they answer back, but only after five or six gins…

Do not move anything

Although the flat may look chaotic, everything has its place, and for a reason. Don't move teddy because he likes sitting on the pouffe, don't move that bowl because it's under the leak, leave those cushions taped to the wall (I bounce off those when I'm stir-crazy).

Don't buy me spontaneous gifts for the home

I know what I like and I'm very fussy. If you buy me a blue spatula it won't go with my red potato masher and these kind of details matter, don't you see ...

Don't laugh at my exercise equipment

Single girls often make rash buys like exercise bikes, rowing machines and Slendertone tummy-reducing belts, which they use once and then leave in a dusty corner so that they can get back to watching videos featuring Andy Garcia.

Lovers beware

When you've left after a night's frolicking, I don't want to find any bits of you left behind: No jockey shorts, shaving foam, football mags, half-eaten burgers or pubic hairs. This is my space and I want to keep it that way, goddam.

FLAT

Here's a list of what a truly badly behaved girl thinks is in and what she thinks is out, what's in and what's out, in and out, in out in out in out in out... sorry, we got carried away there. Basically, whatever the badly behaved girl likes is in – that's the rule. Anyone who says otherwise will get a fat lip.

In things are: Cool, sussed, loose, luscious, fluffy, squelchy, shiny, sequinned, succulent, sugared, caffeinated, 90% proof, 100% bad.

Out things are: Trendy, passé, tight, uptight, arid, raw, sore, chaffing, formica-coated, dry-clean only, 100% nice.

In ✓✓

Lust
Sex
Girl Gangs
Notched bedposts
Slappers
Condom
Condom
Condom
No knickers
Whips & chains
My Hung Like a Donkey
Oxfam
Belly buttons
The "Rachel cut"
Vindaloos
Size 12
Hipsters
Body Hair
Lip Gloss
Swearing
Fags
Window cleaner
Prozac
Horses
Coronation Street
They Think It's All Over
Friends
Wallace & Gromit
Can't Cook Won't Cook
Takeaways
Butter
Hot Dogs
Ketchup
Pizza
Pints
Hair of the dog
Coke

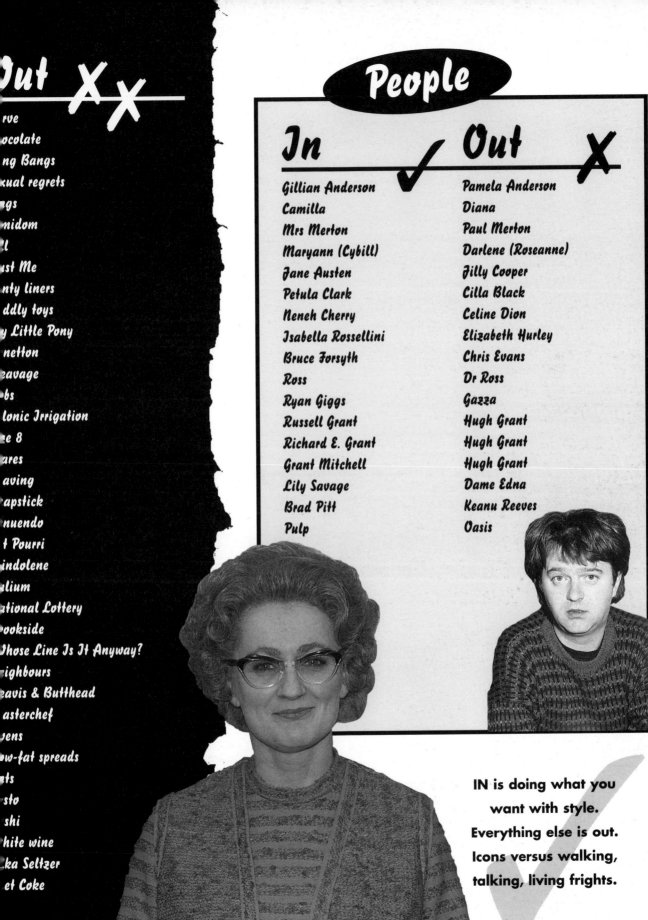

Out ✗✗

...rve
...ocolate
...ng Bangs
...xual regrets
...gs
...nidom
...l
...st Me
...nty liners
...ddly toys
...y Little Pony
...netton
...avage
...bs
...lonic Irrigation
...e 8
...ares
...aving
...apstick
...nuendo
...t Pourri
...indolene
...lium
...ational Lottery
...ookside
...Whose Line Is It Anyway?
...ighbours
...avis & Butthead
...asterchef
...ens
...w-fat spreads
...ts
...sto
...shi
...hite wine
...ka Seltzer
...et Coke

People

In ✓	Out ✗
Gillian Anderson	Pamela Anderson
Camilla	Diana
Mrs Merton	Paul Merton
Maryann (Cybill)	Darlene (Roseanne)
Jane Austen	Jilly Cooper
Petula Clark	Cilla Black
Neneh Cherry	Celine Dion
Isabella Rossellini	Elizabeth Hurley
Bruce Forsyth	Chris Evans
Ross	Dr Ross
Ryan Giggs	Gazza
Russell Grant	Hugh Grant
Richard E. Grant	Hugh Grant
Grant Mitchell	Hugh Grant
Lily Savage	Dame Edna
Brad Pitt	Keanu Reeves
Pulp	Oasis

IN is doing what you want with style. Everything else is out. Icons versus walking, talking, living frights.

Heroines

Madonna

One of the most successful and powerful women of her generation. Nonetheless, she got her kit off for a sub-porn book of photographs. Something most women would only do out of desperate economic necessity.

Margaret Thatcher

Said in 1974, "I owe nothing to Women's Lib", quite rightly recognising the fact that she owed far more to having a millionaire husband. Coincidentally, women in Britain today owe nothing to Margaret Thatcher, who did nothing to help the advancement of women in any area of society, including Parliament. However there is no truth whatsoever in the rumour that she bathes in the blood of virgins.

Jackie Onassis

Married one of the most famous men in the world and then one of the richest. Maintained a dignified and enigmatic silence. Although she was the focus of media attention for decades, was never caught picking her nose in public.

Oprah Winfrey

The original queen of the talk show. Covering important issues of the day such as racism, domestic violence and Claudia Schiffer's exercise video. Her show currently concentrates on how rich Oprah is and how she's not fat any more.

Pamela Anderson

It must be the ultimate ambition for many young women to have a Cola bottle modelled on them. Film star and regular contributor to the documentary series about lifeguards in America, Pammy has proved that plastic breasts get you much further than talent or intellect.

It is very important for the modern girl to have role-models to aspire to and take her example from. It's not actually necessary to shoot all men to make your mark on the world (no matter how attractive that might be), as the following superstars have proved.

The Queen

Richest woman in the world, which is reflected in her style – many coats in pastel shades, with sensible shoes. Despite her public formality, is rumoured to include backgammon and kick-boxing among her hobbies.

Hillary Clinton

The first woman President of the United States (since Nancy Reagan). Hillary realised the key to political success: going blonde, getting contact lenses and wearing pearls. A lesson to us all.

Moira Stuart

Coolest woman in the media. Wears big brooches and jeans behind her newsdesk. Calls everyone at the BBC "babe". So cool she makes Kate Adie look hysterical.

Barbara Cartland

127-year-old novelist and nearly a relative of the royal family. Writes eighty books a week, in which the heroine stays a virgin until she marries. She does not tell you about the subsequent psychosis and eventual violence that ensues when the heroine discovers that her husband has a two-and-a-half-inch penis.

Sister Wendy Beckett

This woman can identify and describe any painting merely by reading the gallery catalogue. And of course Jesus loves her.

Anita Roddick

Founded The Body Shop at a time when the jojoba nut was merely a pipe-dream for most girls. Made it her mission to save the Third World from dry skin.

Princess Diana

Hers was a fairytale story. Married the future king, had two lovely sons, developed bulimia and went to the gym. It was also a fairytale ending, for 17 million reasons.

Wendy Craig

Epitome of '70s motherhood and wifedom. Cornered the market in dippy, frustrated sitcom housewives. Made domestic drudgery acceptable to a whole generation of women.

Lulu

Sang "Shout", married a Bee Gee. Enough said.

Yoko Ono

Sang AAAAAAAAAYYYYYYYEEEEEEEEEE. Married a Beatle. More respect!

All Supermodels

Beauty _is_ skin-deep, and not too much skin at that. We should give thanks to the supermodels for proving that anyone over a size eight is a pig and should stop eating immediately. There are endless financial rewards for being tall, thin and stupid. Special mention to Jodie Kidd, who has set a new standard in female perfection – to lose so much weight that you no longer menstruate.

NEIGHBOURS

EASTENDERS

CORONATION STREET

BROOKSIDE

EMMERDALE

GUIDE TO THE
SOAPS

Long gone are the days of **Dallas** and **Dynasty**, full of wealth, glamour and sex. A wonderful time when lots of ageing actors pretended to be young and raunchy. The budget on these productions was enormous in order to include hairdressers, manicurists, masseurs and an emergency plastic surgeon. Nowadays we have to rely on home-grown (and Australian) soaps to get us into a lather.

NEIGHBOURS

Apart from a couple of token wrinklies, everybody in **Neighbours** is your and gorgeous. All the characters fall deeply in love with each other, split after five minutes, are devastated for three minutes and then fall in love the next person they see. Pretty much like real life really.

TOP RAMSAY STREET TOTTY:

Handyman Sam: Every girl's dream come true. Tall, dark and handsome. Rides motorbike, good at putting up shelves but not too bright.

Stonefish: Crazy name, crazy guy. Against all the odds, "shit for brains" Stonefis Rebecchi managed to go out with future doctor and babe, Cody Willis, **and** get with the stunning Annalise behind Sam's back. Obviously there is more to this du than meets the eye. Within a few short months "Stoney" went from barely literat Neanderthal to poet, songwriter and interpretive dancer. (Forthcoming plot develop ment: he becomes General Secretary of the United Nations and starts a PR agency with Princess Di).

CORONATION STREET

In direct contrast to **Neighbours**, with the occasional exception, nobody in **Coronation Street** is young or sexy. The biggest sex scandal to date has been a love triangle involvingly loathsome Mike Baldwin and Ken and Dreary (sorry, Deirdre) Barlow.

OTHER POSSIBLE CANDIDATES:

Derek Wilton: Not an obvious candidate for sex god. Look closely at Mavis, however, and you will see a constant look of exhaustion.

Des Barnes: has superseded Mike Baldwin as Street philanderer. Face like a bag of chisels, but compared to the rest of the motley crew (Steve & Andy McDonald) a bit of a looker.

EASTENDERS

Set in a fictional East End, which is surely the most depressing wasteland south of the Arctic circle. With so much death and misery, it's hardly surprising that there is constant shagging.

KING SHAGGERS:

Wicks: Sexy man and very cool. Is so committed to shagging every woman in Albert Square that he almost shagged his own daughter (whoops!). Recently caught cavorting with Cindy Beale – wife of his half-brother Ian (super-nerd) Beale.

Grant Mitchell: Big hulking gorilla who is so potent that he has recently made two women on the Square pregnant simply by waving a bar towel at them.

THE BEST LINE UTTERED IN ANY SOAP EVER WAS J.R. TO SUE ELLEN IN *DALLAS*:

" You're a drunk, a tramp and an unfit mother "

*What a role-model for a generation Sue Ellen was. There has never been another woman in a soap who could live up to that wonderful description. Until now. That immortal phrase of JR's could have been written especially for Sammy Rogers of Brookside. What a girl! Gorgeous, drunk, cheap and totally irresponsible. She made the silly mistake of getting married (for goodness sake) at the peak of her sexiness, but just when we thought she was lost forever to panto land, she came back and behaved like a total slut. **Fantastic.***

BROOKSIDE

All the men in **Brookside** have faces like a bullfrog that's just been stung by a wasp, so it's left to a girl to save the day.

EMMERDALE

N.B. It doesn't matter how many lesbian lovers, extra-marital affairs and muscles you cram in. A farm is a farm is a farm.

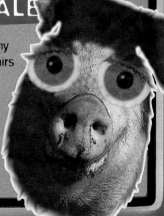

GIRLS

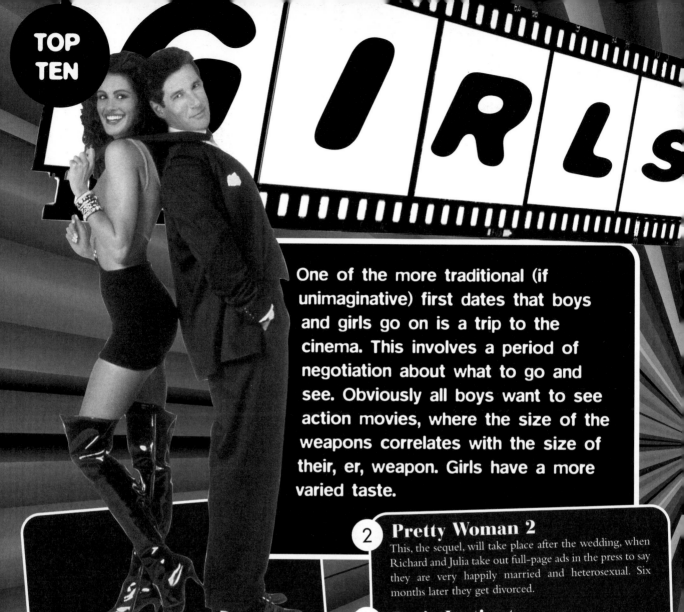

One of the more traditional (if unimaginative) first dates that boys and girls go on is a trip to the cinema. This involves a period of negotiation about what to go and see. Obviously all boys want to see action movies, where the size of the weapons correlates with the size of their, er, weapon. Girls have a more varied taste.

1 Pretty Woman

It is a wonderful thing for us girls to have strong role models to instil us with a sense of ambition and self-respect. A task performed particularly well by Julia Roberts in this modern-day Cinderella tale. Obviously selling your body for sex is something most of us can only aspire to. But it is worth persevering with your dream, because inevitably after a short period of walking the streets late at night, one of the kerb-crawlers you pick up will be a handsome millionaire. He, of course, will look beyond the perfunctory nature of the relationship and see the true romance of the situation.

Where the film lets all right-minded girls down is when Richard Gere offers to get Julia an apartment, give her credit cards and then come round for a shag from time to time. She should of course have taken his hand off. What a fantastic deal! However, she will accept nothing less than marriage. It is at this point that the film loses the illusion of reality that it has thus far admirably maintained.

2 Pretty Woman 2

This, the sequel, will take place after the wedding, when Richard and Julia take out full-page ads in the press to say they are very happily married and heterosexual. Six months later they get divorced.

3 Basic Instinct

The scene in the disco alone makes this film worth seeing. The hilarious sight of the repulsive 50-year-old Michael Douglas attempting to shake his funky stuff and re-introducing the tight-fitting fawn-coloured sweater as a fashion must. Also to be considered is the wonderfully realistic portrayal of a lesbian as a Barbie Doll serial-killer. But who could forget the infamous Sharon Stone flash-the-gash scene – the Hollywood equivalent of accidentally tucking your skirt into the back of your knickers.

4 Fatal Attraction

An excellent cautionary tale for all modern single women. The lesson to be learned is that you can't have a casual shag without becoming totally obsessed with the guy, losing your mind and boiling his rabbit. Even if you are careful enough to choose someone as deeply unattractive as Michael Douglas (again!) you are bound to end up dead in the bath and it will all be your own fault.

FILMS

5 Four Weddings & a Funeral
(or Five Funerals, depending on your point of view)
The central message of this film appears to be that if you haven't found your partner for life by the time you are thirty, you're finished. Now, given that most mornings it's hard enough to find your shoes, we'd better buck up our ideas.

6 Ghost
All together now, "Oh ma lurve, ma darlin' ." Demi Moore makes love to a mound of clay, understandably mistaking it for hubby Patrick Swayze. He dies satisfyingly early in the film. She cries a bit and then gets off with Whoopi Goldberg, whom she understandably mistakes for hubby Patrick Swayze... and they all live happily ever after. Except Patrick and the bloke who had him killed, who also dies.

7 Forrest Gump
If your mother went round all day saying things like, "Life is like a box of chocolates", you'd have her put into residential care, bless her. Not in this film, though. Here she is, a paragon of all-American wisdom. Forrest swallows all the wholesome apple-pie ideals/right-wing bigotry of his mother and spouts off at everyone he meets. Rather than being the nerd who is destined to end up keeping pigeons and talking to his feet, Forrest is saved by the fact that he can run fast. That ability, plus his enthusiasm for imperialist warfare, makes him a hero. The girl he loves is a liberated woman who makes her own choices, therefore she must die, but not before Forrest magnanimously forgives her for not being like his mum.

8 Terms of Endearment
The ultimate tear-jerker. Debra Winger has a bullying mother, marries a feeble cheating bastard, stays barefoot, pregnant and in the kitchen, gets cancer, spends her last days trying to pacify her selfish mother, husband, friend and bratty son, then dies. Jack Nicholson plays it for laughs.

9 Truly, Madly, Deeply
Or, to give it its proper title, Truly Badly Awful. Juliet Stephenson's pompous bore of a boyfriend dies. Everyone else in the known universe falls in love with her. His ghost turns up, trashes her house and leaves again. She cries a lot, then she skips a bit.

10 Home Alone
What we really wanted to see was that revolting 8-year-old, five minutes after his family left him on his own, looking for his presents but finding the bleach. Drinking it and dying.

Anything by Merchant Ivory
Oh yes. There is nothing that girls enjoy more than watching a period costume melodrama set in a country house, where absolutely nothing at all happens apart from the odd sigh of restrained passion. The height of rebellion is always Helena Bonham-Carter letting her hair loose for five minutes. All filmed through industrial-strength gauze, which can just about make Emma Thompson look pretty. About as interesting as watching grass grow, which coincidentally is what most of the characters do for most of the film.

Some girls have it, some girls don't. Some achieve it effortlessly and men and women watch in awe, while others inspire the pity and derision usually reserved for Whitney Houston's better attempts at soul. You can't buy it and you can't fake it. It's called attitude.

GIRLS WITH ATTITU

COURTNEY LOVE

Well, anyone who calls their band Hole, and applies her lipstick so badly she gives beauticians sleepless nights, is OK by us. Had a baby and refused to stay at home discussing nappies, sending social services into a spin.

ELIZABETH THE FIRST

Top woman, queen, great hair, never married, beheaded sleazeballs. Not to be confused with present-day namesake: queen, crap hair, married sleazeball.

SUSAN SARANDON

Got to be a Hollywood actress despite resembling everyone's mad auntie. Gave the archetypal girl-next-door some boot in *The Rocky Horror Picture Show* and later did lots of cheer-along shooting in the excellent *Thelma and Louise*. She says what she thinks and looks like she knows how to drink. As a role model? Well...driving, shooting and drinking. What more could a girl do in a weekend?

Historically you can trace it back to various heroines who weren't afraid to get their hands bloody or their boyfriends slaughtered (and not necessarily down the pub). The following are to be seen as icons, rather than role models (unless you want to model yourself on them).

DE

SPICE GIRLS

These newcomers show signs of being our kind of gals. If the press puff can be believed, they like to be in control and won't take the music-business boys' club shit lying down (as is expected of women in that world, preferably with legs akimbo). Unlike Shampoo, who try too hard and miss the mark, you could imagine going for a drink with Spice (and a curry). Shampoo, chuck the little-girl hairslides and hit the vodka.

HELEN OF TROY

Well, she wasn't bad-looking, but it was a bit much causing a 10-year war over the basic "you looking at my bird" -type pub brawl. No, there is a bit more to this than history would have us believe. She was playing the classic holding-out game. "Paris, go and fight Achilles and when you come back, I might let you touch it..."

ROSEANNE

Writer, comedian and actor. For her ever-popular sitcom she hires and fires her puny male writers at will. She refused to be typecast as either little woman or kooky sidekick, which means she is considered difficult. When translated out of Hollywood-speak this means she's a girl behaving very badly indeed. What's more – don't you just know a Slimfast has never slipped past those luscious lips.

THE QUEEN OF SHEBA

An all-round hot patootie. Brought sex to Solomon, whose Oprah-type dilemma was the first of its kind to feature in the Old Testament. "I'm very studious and religious, but I've met a more experienced woman who's taught me that there's more to life than books. I don't want to lose my seat in Heaven, but I can't say no." Saucy Sheba annoyed God by challenging his authority – no wonder he chose a virgin to be the mother of Jesus.

> COME ON, GIRLS, GRAB YOUR BOWS AND ARROWS, WE'RE GOING UP WEST.

> 'ERE, PUT DOWN THAT GOBLET OF MALIBU AND STAB THAT ROMAN GEEZER. YOU MIGHT EVEN GET LUCKY WITH ONE OF THEM – THEY **ARE** ITALIAN.

Bad

BE

Boadicea

The great Celtic queen who defeated the Roman army because she didn't want Britain to be part of Europe. Apparently Boadicea hailed from Essex, so it's easy to imagine her in a bearskin mini, a pair of wooden stilettos, a frizzy perm and dancing on a Saturday night with her mates round their spears.

Catherine the Great, Empress of Russia

Cath was a leading light in political reform. She founded several schools for girls and a medical college to provide health care for her subjects. She was intelligent and well acquainted with French literature, but despite her benevolent achievements, she is still best remembered for allegedly kopping off with one of her general's horses, thus doing herself untold internal damage and causing her untimely death. There's a motto here: No matter how horny you are, stick to your own species - horses never take off their shoes and have terrible breath.

Queen Caroline (George IV's wife)

By all accounts, a grotesque creature with no shame and few inhibitions. She was renowned for not wearing any panties, then lifting her skirt in mixed company and shrieking, "Look, look, my fanny!" Word has it that she bore so many illegitimate children that she took to birthing herself, wrapping the tot in swaddling and leaving it on her own doorstep before ringing the bell. She would nip back inside and feign total ignorance when told of its existence. The child would be taken in and brought up as one of the family without anyone suspecting a thing.

Anne Boleyn

Poor Anne was accused of adultery with several dukes and lords, including her own brother! She was beheaded like so many of Henry's ex's, leaving her bulbous husband free to wed again. But let's be honest, you'd have to be crazy to marry Henry the Eighth! It would be like marrying O J Simpson. Imagine breaking the news to your mum.

Cleopatra

By all accounts, an exquisitely beautiful woman. She ignored all advice when it came to hairstyles and invented her own look. She was a bit of a Goth when it came to make-up and preferred her jewellery big and resting on her cleavage. At a time when Rome was invading and conquering most of the world, she decided to take things into her own hands and save Egypt by allowing both the Emperor Julius Caesar and his commander, Mark Antony to invade her instead. Just lie back and think of Egypt was her motto. She met her end when a poisonous snake grew fed up with her nasty girl act and bit her. Quite what the reptile was doing in her bedchamber with a pair of trousers on has never come to light.

Calamity Jane

So called because she threatened that calamity would befall any man who offended her. She dressed as a bloke, smoked cigars for breakfast and could tame a wild stallion in under a minute. She worked as a scout for the cavalry, which did not mean tying knots and singing "Ging Gang Goolee" around the campfire. No, she had a very high-risk job, which involved riding ahead to check that the area was safe from marauding Indians and avoiding getting scalped on the way back. She was a dab hand with a rifle and her party trick was catching bullets between her teeth and spitting them out at cowboys. She toured as a stand-up comic who could crack a mean whip and drank neat whisky twenty-four hours a day. In 1891 she settled down and married a cab driver who was prepared to go south of the river, and further.

Ruth Ellis

A truly trashy blonde with a great capacity for booze, toy-boys and expensive accessories. She began her sleazy career as a photographer's model, before becoming a hostess in a private drinking club. She bore two children to two different men and fell in love with a notorious drunken womaniser with a reputation as a mummy's boy. He beat and bullied her and, when he failed to turn up for a date, she drank a gallon of gin, borrowed a gun from her sugar daddy and killed him. She was often heard remarking, "that bleedin' David's doin' my head in, I swear I'll swing for him one day". Sounds perfectly reasonable.

HEALTH ANDFITNESS

The only reason to take any form of physical exercise is to look as fit as a butcher's dog so that you can shag anyone you want to. The most irritating thing about gyms are the sassy, cute little girlie teachers who shout commands and try to shame you

into becoming thin. A word of advice – always choose a class given by a spunky male instructor. That way, when you're punishing yourself with agonising sit-ups and buttock clenches, you can at least fantasise about having mad, bad, passionate sex with the instructor.

Leg-spreading machines are especially popular amongst single females. But do make sure your trusty Lycra leotard can be trusted. If it shifts too far to one side, it may expose wads of thick pubic hair, which is not a pretty sight.

Most gyms have TV sets tuned into MTV. Usually there is some gorgeous hunk or ripe boy band belting out tunes, so just concentrate on the screen and imagine anything your heart desires. You'll forget all about the pain, and at the same time tone those flabby muscles. But don't get too carried away – an orgasm in public is neither ladylike nor socially acceptable.

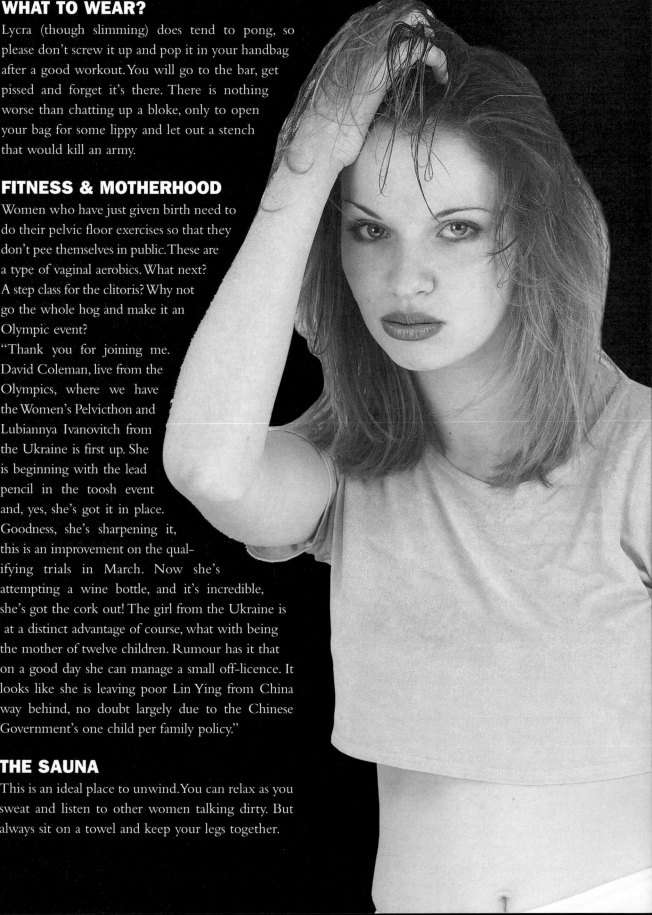

WHAT TO WEAR?

Lycra (though slimming) does tend to pong, so please don't screw it up and pop it in your handbag after a good workout. You will go to the bar, get pissed and forget it's there. There is nothing worse than chatting up a bloke, only to open your bag for some lippy and let out a stench that would kill an army.

FITNESS & MOTHERHOOD

Women who have just given birth need to do their pelvic floor exercises so that they don't pee themselves in public. These are a type of vaginal aerobics. What next? A step class for the clitoris? Why not go the whole hog and make it an Olympic event?

"Thank you for joining me. David Coleman, live from the Olympics, where we have the Women's Pelvicthon and Lubiannya Ivanovitch from the Ukraine is first up. She is beginning with the lead pencil in the toosh event and, yes, she's got it in place. Goodness, she's sharpening it, this is an improvement on the qual– ifying trials in March. Now she's attempting a wine bottle, and it's incredible, she's got the cork out! The girl from the Ukraine is at a distinct advantage of course, what with being the mother of twelve children. Rumour has it that on a good day she can manage a small off-licence. It looks like she is leaving poor Lin Ying from China way behind, no doubt largely due to the Chinese Government's one child per family policy."

THE SAUNA

This is an ideal place to unwind. You can relax as you sweat and listen to other women talking dirty. But always sit on a towel and keep your legs together.

VIBRATOR

WHY SPEND THE DAY CONSTANTLY PICKING UP, PUTTING AWAY, LOSING, FINDING AND LOSING AGAIN ALL THOSE DIFFERENT HOUSEHOLD OBJECTS THAT HELP YOU THROUGH THOSE LONG HOUSEWIFELY DAYS. WE SAY BANISH THOSE BUGGERS TO THE UTILITY ROOM, BECAUSE ALL YOU NEED IS ONE OBJECT ALONE.

A DAY IN THE LIFE OF A GIRL'S BEST FRIEND!

THERE IS NOTHING MORE APPRECIATED THAN POPPING SOMETHING TASTY AND NOURISHING INTO YOUR MOUTH FIRST THING IN THE MORNING. JUST SET THE VIBRATOR TO SPIN AND SEE HOW QUICKLY THOSE ORANGES ARE JUICED.

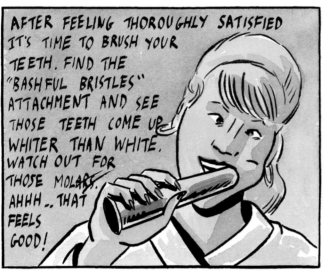

AFTER FEELING THOROUGHLY SATISFIED IT'S TIME TO BRUSH YOUR TEETH. FIND THE "BASHFUL BRISTLES" ATTACHMENT AND SEE THOSE TEETH COME UP WHITER THAN WHITE. WATCH OUT FOR THOSE MOLARS. AHHH... THAT FEELS GOOD!

BEFORE LEAVING THE BATHROOM, GOT TO GIVE THAT OLD EAR WAX A GOOD BASHING... OOOH... THERE WE ARE!

WHO'S THAT AT THE BOTTOM OF THE STAIRS?

THAT'S RIGHT IT'S FIDO WANTING TO PLAY.

OKAY BOY...
...FETCH.

OH HOW HE LOVES THE FEEL OF THAT LONG HARD OBJECT BETWEEN HIS TEETH. DON'T CHEW TOO HARD BOY.

9:30 a.m.

TIME FOR MORE WOMENS WORK (IT'S NEVER DONE). OH NO! THE HOOVER'S ALL BLOCKED UP.

WHAT CAN YOU UNCLOG IT WITH? WHERE'S THAT TRUSTY VIBRATOR? FITS PERFECTLY.

THAT'S BETTER, ALL LOOSE AND...

... ABLE TO CONTINUE SUCKING.

AT LAST IT'S TIME FOR LUNCH, WHO FANCIES A BIG TASTY HOT DOG TO FILL THEM UP INSIDE? BUT HOW DO YOU GET THE HOLE IN THE BUN? THAT'S RIGHT IT'S JUST SO VERSATILE. BETTER USE THE "POINTY POINTY" EXTENSION OR IT MIGHT NOT GO IN SMOOTHLY.

AFTER LUNCH TURN YOUR HANDS SPOT OF GREEN FINGER WORK GARDENING. IF YOUR BOX IS A BIT EMPTY AND NEEDS A BEDDING PLANTS PANSIES DO THE TRICK. IN...OUT..IN... TO A LOOKING FEW SHOULD ..OUT..THERE A HOLE..

...BIG ENOUGH TO PUT IN YOUR NEW PLANTS.

11:30 pm. ONE OF THE WONDERFUL THINGS ABOUT YOUR TRUSTY DILDO IS THAT AFTER USING IT TO STIR THE COCOA TILL IT'S NICE AND FROTHY...

...YOU CAN USE IT TO STIR YOURSELF...

...AND SO TO BED.

Real-Life Magazines

USUALLY found in doctors' surgeries or the homes of depressed housewives. These are fantastic for great tales of bad, bad behaviour, because almost any issue contains a veritable diary of lewd and rude titbits. They have titillating titles such as:

"I've got two vaginas and I intend to use them both!"

"My boss sacked me, so I put a freshly killed mouse in his cheese bap!"

"Something wet and slimy landed on my flip flops so I married him!"

• They are chocca with true-life tragedies, ranging from bulimia to penis whittling (a popular pastime in the United States of America).

• They have easier-than-easy competitions such as:

"Here's a pic of Englebert Humperdinck and here's one of Linda Lusardi. Can you tell us which one was once a Page 3 girl?"

• Ideal for those moody-blue days when you're feeling fat, ugly and suicidal – just flick through and you will instantly feel normal and on top of the world.

Women's magazines are most commonly leafed through at dentists and hairdressing salons, setting lifestyle standards and sharing showbiz gossip with all who read them. They come in an assortment of publications, and give much advice on how to behave and how not to.

The Glossies

Magazines like *Elle* and *Marie Claire* are a must for the fashion-conscious. There's always a feature on impoverished women of the Third World, so that we can feel guilty at having enough spare dosh to buy the bleedin' magazine in the first place and at the same time empathise with their tragic plight and be able to comment knowledgeably at swanky dinner parties.

Hello! Magazine

Hot gossip amongst the rich and famous. Princess Diana is the most featured "lovely", closely followed by Fergie, Jane Seymour and Sharon Stone. Centrefold spreads depicting the lavish homes of little-known countesses with bad face-lifts are their special-

ity. It is alleged that *Hello!* has its very own curse: a high percentage of celebrity newly-weds who rake in piles of cash by sharing their big day with the magazine wind up in the divorce courts. Perhaps the magazine should be renamed *Bye Bye*.

It's a pity that *Hello!* magazine wasn't around in Tudor times to publish a feature on King Henry VIII and his wives.

****** E X C L U S I V E ! ******
"Henry VIII shows **Hello!** *around his new home at Hampton Court where he holds the biggest balls in Europe. Our well-loved monarch is accompanied by his gorgeous new bride, a pretty young girl with a good head on her shoulders."*

Horoscopes

Always full of good news, no matter what star sign you are. Complete and utter bollocks, but we keep reading them. We generally tend to read our ex's sign for years after breaking up, hoping to read encouraging forecasts such as "killed in horrific car accident, record collection is yours".

Horoscope pages also tell you which celebrities you share your birthday with – perhaps you were born on the same day as Anthea Turner? So if everybody forgets the special day and you wind up all alone and sad, drowning your sorrows with a can of Special Brew still in its brown paper bag, you can at least think about Anthea and feel even more depressed. Of course, looking on the bright side, you may share your birthday with a dead celeb and at least you're alive, so that's one up on them.

TAMPAX & T

Tampons are still a luxury item, according to the wise men of Whitehall. So if you're fed up of paying VAT on vaginal necessities, tax on tampons and loads of dosh on your one-way dry-weave top sheet, then here are a few tips for rolling your own.

TAMPON REPLACEMENTS

1 KITCHEN ROLL
(unrolled) – heavy flow

2 COTTON BUD
light flow

3 NAVEL FLUFF
extra light flow

4 SMALL PERSIAN CAT
(preferably white & declawed) for the woman who wants an extra pussy

5 A BANANA

TOWEL REPLACEMENTS

1 KITCHEN ROLL
(rolled)

2 SLIGHTLY BIGGER PERSIAN PUSSY
(with claws for extra security)

3 PITTA BREAD
(untoasted)

4 HOUSE BRICK

5 BRILLO PAD

6 PILLOW

TAMPONS

A COMPANY that can't be named is to launch a new tampon in the new year. The tampon is shaped like a flower, which blossoms after it is inserted. Suggested names have been "Fanny Flowers" and "Daffodil in my knickers", but these are just working titles.

THERE ARE TO BE THREE TYPES:

1 LIGHT FLOW CROCUS
2 MEDIUM FLOW TULIP
3 HEAVY FLOW   CHELSEA FLOWER SHOW

There are two potential problems with these new tampons. The first is the obvious pollination problem, and the heavier the period, the more bees you are likely to attract.

The second problem is a little more delicate. The manufacturers tested the tampons on members of staff in their factory and the tampons were found to give these women spontaneous orgasms. This confused the male members of the company, as they had never heard the words "spontaneous" and "orgasm" used in the same sentence, let alone witnessed its event.

At this point the working title was changed to "Finishing the job" and "Ha... Ha... Ha... Ha... Ha...!!!!!!!"

Women in the factory began to look forward to their periods and men became threatened, hence the "Fanny Flower" will never see the shelves in our shops or indeed the walls of our uterus. And for us, the general public, the spontaneous orgasm in Sainsbury's will eventually become a myth, and men can once again feel safe in the knowledge that saying it with flowers indicates nothing more that potential hayfever.

Wonder

With the invention of the Wonderbra, every woman can now have boobs that look as though the laws of gravity have been defied. Although every woman (or man – we don't want to be sexist) now has the right and the means to have a cleavage, the Wonderbra is not necessarily the best thing since the eighteen-hour girdle.

The Wonderbra can be a very scary item indeed. We tried some on recently, only to find that our boobs had disappeared and in replacement we had a couple more double-chins. Still, we found them handy when on a long journey and in need of a travel cushion. Very comfy!

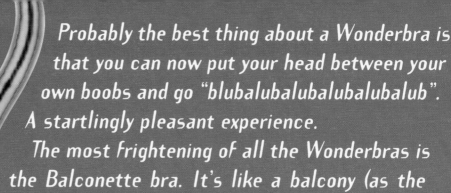

Probably the best thing about a Wonderbra is that you can now put your head between your own boobs and go "blubalubalubalubalubalub". A startlingly pleasant experience.

The most frightening of all the Wonderbras is the Balconette bra. It's like a balcony (as the name suggests) for your boobs. Looking down is very frightening, however... You can eat your lunch off your boobs, but be careful if you're eating chicken breasts – we don't want to get confused, do we? After all, we are only girls and confusion is a way of life for us. (That was irony, in case any feminists are getting upset.)

Other Handy Uses for the Wonderbra

1	Handcuffs	6	Jockstrap
2	Hanging plant pots	7	Sanitary towel
3	Haemorrhoid cushion	8	Brain-teaser (for men)
4	Bouncy castle	9	Bib
5	Double hammock	10	Nose bag.

KNICKERS

Whatever you call them – knickers, panties, undies – these small pieces of material are a fascination to men worldwide from a very early age. (We all know about hiding in your bedroom with your mum's catalogue.) Knickers form a closer, more intimate relationship with your crotch than most men ever dream of, adding to the fear and envy of GIRLS' PANTS. But how can you tell who's wearing what? Generally you can't. The most outrageous women feel more at home in your cotton comfy undies, whereas the shyest of Mother Superiors could be sporting the latest leather thong. There is a wide variety of undergarments on the market. Here are just a few...

The Basic Bikini

Generally purchased at Marks & Spencer and in packs of six. They are *always* made from cotton, anything else just isn't cricket. These are the Ford Escort of the knicker world, popular, reliable and common, but after six months become boring and tacky, leaving you wanting new ones.

The Girly Basic

Like the basic (above left) with a few frilly bits. Could be used as a puller (above left), if you're trying to get off with Mr Nice/potential father of your children, but otherwise use only for days when you want to be secure in the fact that you have something pretty against your bits. WARNING: Check the frills before purchasing. They tend to be a bit itchy, especially around the gusset seam area.

The Puller

This is for serious copping off only. This tiny excuse for a pair of pants will barely cover your pubes, so hair removal from your entire pubic area beforehand is essential (and painful). The sides are constructed from cotton thread for easy ripping off and there's no reinforced gusset in this one as, hopefully, they won't be on long enough to need one. Variations are transparent, edible or G-string. Use the latter only if you enjoy the sensation of having your bottom sliced in two.

The Period Knicker

There are various types of period knickers: a) white basics that escaped into the dark wash; b) the new fad of low-cut, high-waisted, tummy-reducing (ha! that's a laugh) pants that make you look pregnant and incontinent; c) all others that became period knickers at the beginning of previous periods. (Generally accompanied by the phrase "oh fuck".) One of the unfortunate things about period panties is that sod's law means you are wearing them when you actually pull.

The Knicker Shorts

Only the positively anorexic can get away with wearing these without looking like an overgrown schoolgirl on sports day. For the very flattest of stomachs only. If you buy them thinking "ooh, they look comfy", then you are sadly mistaken. With the lack of any sign of a gusset, the prominent seam running from your naval all the way down and back up the other side gives the G-string effect, only this time it includes your clitoris (Mmm, comfy). This is fine if you enjoy feeling like a piece of Edam on a cheese slicer, but personally we'd prefer something else rubbing up and down our bits. (Like Johnny Depp, perhaps.)

The BIG Knickers

BIG knickers are strictly live-alone, night-in (or have been married a very long time) knickers. They are the size of a small country and have a gusset the size of Dorset, reinforced with the National Guard. Made from duvet material, they give maximum security. No need to pull, tug, adjust or itch, just pull these pants up to your neck and relax (remembering never to answer the door).

LOSING KNICKERS

Women are *always* buying knickers, yet have you ever suddenly needed an extra room, just for your pants? Not so far. *Where do they go?* Who gets home from a busy day, walks in the door and suddenly realises that they've left their knickers at work *again*? Even after a particularly great, heavy petting session, you're not likely to return without your pants every time. A few occasions is fine, but if it is happening on a regular basis, it's time to reassess your lifestyle. In the past women would leave earrings behind so that men would have to call. Is the '90s equivalent leaving knickers behind?

If you are seriously considering this, think again. They're more likely to end up over the bar at his local. There are two explanations for the disappearance of knickers:
1) The Knicker Thief, a bit like the tooth fairy, except it goes into your drawers (the wooden variety, of course). 2) The Knicker Planet, a bit like the odd sock planet, a mystery that shall never be solved.

Girls and

ENVIRONMENT

At the beginning of each new season the woman leaves her nest and commences the prowl. With stalking eyes, camouflaged in easy-to-remove attire and armed with bag and purse, she heads for the nearest mall or High Street. It is here, in her natural environment, that the woman's senses come alive. Travelling sometimes up to ten miles in one day, she detects her prey by sight or touch, stealing up to within three to five metres of it before making a sudden rush from behind. Grasping the item, she then repeats the process several times.

£89.00

vicious

Once fully loaded, with adrenalin pumping through her veins, she heads with one swift movement to the changing room. Often she will have too many items. In this case she will know that only three may be allowed at one time. She will then leave the remaining items with another woman – the shop assistant. There may often be more than one shop assistant; these are generally found huddled together, either dancing to music or chatting amongst themselves. These types of women are the most vicious of the species.

£150.00

naked

In the changing room there are many other women of all shapes and sizes, standing in front of rectangular reflective glass, and it is here that many will decide to change their diet. The behaviour patterns of the woman are perhaps at their most interesting here. Shedding last year's garments, she skilfully covers her near-naked form with her catch. Eyes fixed on her reflection, she is now at her most focused. If the garment is not to her liking, the woman swiftly tears it off and throws it to the floor. Only when one suits her build and appearance will the woman's face break into a smile. This may take many hours to achieve. It is now that the woman may hum along to the background music and parade her new feathers.

Shopping

COFFEE

If the woman has high-heeled shoes, her pain threshold will be lower than that of her flat-toed friends. She will need to replenish herself with a cup of coffee and possibly a doughnut. Often she will meet up with other women and, until nightfall, will continue the shopping process in packs.

Stamina

THE SHOPPING PROCESS IS THE WOMAN'S GREATEST DISPLAY OF STAMINA AND SURVIVAL. IT CAN BE OBSERVED DAILY IN SHOPPING CENTRES ALL OVER THE WORLD.

£45.00

FORNICATION

On return to her lair, the woman will become anxious, often hiding her catch behind her back while she checks the mood of her mate. A feast may be prepared by the woman before displaying her day's work. When all is well, they will lie down together and there starts the fornication process (see Reproduction).

Girls We Love to Hate!

Being a girl is a wonderful thing – there's no doubt that women are much, much better than men at everything. But there are always a few silly old birds who let the side down, and these are the girls we love to hate. Here is a list of those foolish females who get on our flippin' nerves.

GABY ROSLIN

For being too blonde, too cheerful and too nice. If Gaby would wear a PVC corset, get a few tattoos and insult all of her interviewees, we might be able to bear watching her.

TANIA BRYER

Who the hell is she and why is she always in *Hello*? A so-called TV presenter (who's never on the telly), who spends all her time queening around at various up-market social functions with sundry braying hoorays in tow.

ALL THE ACTRESSES IN *FRIENDS*

For looking as if they were hand-picked by a marketing man (one blonde, one brunette, one dark) and for sharing and caring with three adorable men, who resemble the men in our lives as much as chalk resembles cheese.

PAULA YATES

For letting the side down by flirting with everything in trousers, playing the victim in her separation from Bob, and calling her children dippy names that will stigmatise the poor little devils for life. Then she goes bragging about her exceptional IQ. I think not.

...because all our boyfriends go "Aaaah!" when they see her elfin cuteness, and we wanted her to be our own girl-woman screechy-doll.

PATSY KENSIT

For being the pretty little appendage to a series of rock-lads, in particular Liam, whose repulsive slobbishness means she must be a Grade A masochist. Added annoyance: he's very rich, a great singer and when you see her interviewed, she seems quite sane.

ULRIKA JONSSON

For being everywhere on account of having been a weather girl and having a bottle of peroxide.

ANTHEA TURNER

For her fatuous smile, prissy feathery haircut and limp persona. Deserves a good smacking.

KATE MOSS

For being so young, so thin and so contemptuous. Plus she had sex with Johnny Depp.

CLAUDIA SCHIFFER

For being hatefully beautiful and for letting ugly blokes like that magician think they stand a chance. We want our princesses to mate with princes.

DEMI MOORE

Dead ordinary actress who's somehow made herself the highest-paid woman in Hollywood by appearing in a bunch of terrible films in which she always gets her kit off. Added annoyance: she's very happily married...

A girl's guide to computers

Before we start, remember this is technical stuff and should only be attempted in the presence of something male. A man is good, but a dog or gerbil will suffice.

RAM

It is important to check the size of your RAM. The more RAM a man has, the better (no change there). Four meg of RAM won't get you very far. You really need eight or twelve meg of RAM (unless you're in Wales, when you're in trouble) to really feel the force of your machine. Be careful that your computer doesn't go down on you. It may be strangely pleasurable, but you will lose both your memory and your RAM. (There are other sorts of RAM, e.g. VRAM DRAM, that you don't have to worry your pretty little heads about. But one not to mention in front of a man is PRAM.)

hard drives & hardware floppy disks

HARD DRIVES, HARDWARE AND FLOPPY DISKS

Men have been known regularly to mount their hard drives into soft partitions. It is only then that they can play with their hardware or, if tha fails, then their floppy disks. Worryingly, floppy disks are getting smaller. Five years ago the average size of a man's floppy was five and a quarter inches, whereas now it has shrunk to a meagre three and a half. Maybe this is why jo sticks have become more popular with the girls

HOW TO LAND A TECHNO-NERD (SEE ANORAK)

This isn't as bad as it sounds. Bill Gates, while not being much of a looker, has a throbbing bank account and as much RAM as you can handle in a lifetime. (But you're more likely to get multi-media than multi-orgasms with old Billy Boy).

Chat-up lines for a nerd:
"Oops! I think I just sat on your interface?"
"Wow, you've got an enormous package!"
"Thanks for the memory."

WHERE TO FIND YOURSELF A TECHNO-NERD
The Cyber Café

Basically a coffee house for geeks. Try slinking over to your off-guard geek, putting your hand on his joystick and asking if you can play with his peripheral. This may be greeted with the opening of his anorak so that he can take out his floppy, but persevere until he asks you to find his zip file, when you can finally fly off into cyberspace together.

The Internet

The Internet is no relation to the fishnet. One is a sexy stocking used for pulling lads and the other is some sort of a packet-switching protocol, very long words coming from a blonde. If you meet a man over the Internet (as opposed to over his desk), he is likely to be very good with his fingers – after all, typing endlessly on his keyboard has got to have some advantages.

Having said this, *never* meet up with someone you've met via the Internet – it'll only lead to misery. No matter how fast he can touch-type, those fingers will always be attached to his keyboard and he'll only have eyes for his monitor (not his milk monitor, unless he's some kind of perv, which is possible). Even if he tells you that he looks like Brad Pitt (he's much more likely to resemble Brad's kid brother Ces), and boasts about his 16 meg of RAM, just check out his porn connection bill. That way you really will know if he wants to mount his hard drive or you.

HE MOUSE
bit of plastic that looks
othing like a mouse and
es something.

*Such an anti climax –
the 3½" floppy.*

Dieting is an early form of female torture, introduced by Belgian nuns in the early twelfth Century to give themselves fainting fits and hallucinations, which they thought brought them closer to God. We modern girls dabble in this ritual self-abuse when we wish to:

- Waste our money to experience humbleness.
- Understand and celebrate human weakness.
- Philosophize on the pointlessness of human endeavour.
- Keep our minds on the higher spiritual plane of magical diet tips, marvellous slimming tricks with stripes, hairstyles that deflect attention from ruddy chipmunk cheeks, and vital updates on the very narrow weight-range and body-type that the fashionable man could possibly consider fuckable and, more importantly, marriageable.

TRY TO CHOOSE FOODS THAT ARE HIGH IN FLAVOUR AND LOW IN CALORIES, USING THIS HANDY CHART:

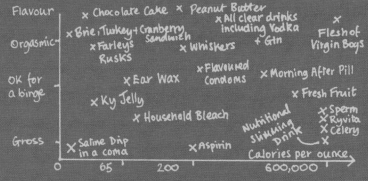

Flavour — ✗ Chocolate Cake ✗ Peanut Butter
Orgasmic — ✗ Brie, Turkey + Cranberry Sandwich ✗ All clear drinks including Vodka + Gin ✗ Farleys Rusks ✗ Whiskers ✗ Flesh of Virgin Boys
OK for a binge — ✗ Ear Wax ✗ Flavoured Condoms ✗ Morning After Pill ✗ Ky Jelly ✗ Fresh Fruit ✗ Household Bleach ✗ Nutritional Slimming Drink ✗ Sperm ✗ Ryvita ✗ Celery
Gross — ✗ Saline Drip in a coma ✗ Aspirin ✗

Calories per ounce
0   65   200   600,000

1% WHOLE FAMILY KILLED IN FREAK PENGUIN ATTACK

10% A LULL IN THE CONVERSATION

10% CHILDREN ARE STARVING IN AFRICA BUT IT WOULD GO OFF BY THE TIME IT GOT THER

10% THE TELEVISION IS BROKEN

5% YOU'RE NOT CLAUDIA SCHIFFER

5% YOU HAVEN'T GOT A COCK IN YOUR MOUTH

5% THE VOICES IN YOUR HEAD TOLD YOU TO

CELEBRITY DIETS	THE PRINCESS DIET	THE KAREN CARPENTER DIET	THE KATE MOSS DIET	THE ELIZABETH TAYLOR DIET
DETAILS	Marry royalty. Exercise a lot – you have nothing else to do. Cling desperately to ex-husband's prestige.	Eat 2 boxes of laxatives a day. Form a music duo with your brother.	Have a really difficult job that involves existing and walking. Have a totally unaddictive, uninteresting personality.	Binge on painkillers, booze, husbands and kaftans. Dry out in a clinic and repeat annu
RESULTS	Significant weight loss, with inability to sit up straight and focus. Be so annoying you get paid £30 million to sling your hook.	Bad sex life. Significant weight loss from heart attack, and death.	You're born slim, you stay slim and briefly personify the waif-like look which has zero sex appeal.	Wild weight fluctuati which are well photo graphed so that peopl can compare photos disgusted awe and gle

Diets

Comfort eating is often a major cause of weight gain - this chart shows you the most common causes so that you can be extra vigilant at these times.

39% THE FOOD WAS ASKING FOR IT

15% YOU JUST LOOKED IN THE MIRROR

SOME MAGICAL DIET TIPS

SMOKE, DRINK, TAKE DRUGS AND BONK LIKE A BUNNY.

ALWAYS GO AROUND WITH A FAT FRIEND.

SCOOP YOUR STOMACH UP INTO YOUR WONDERBRA AND FASHION ANY EXCESS FLESH NOT NEEDED FOR YOUR CLEAVAGE INTO A CHOKER AROUND YOUR NECK, PAINT IT GOLD AND VARNISH IT.

EAT SIXTY SMALL MEALS A DAY.

EAT A HEARTY MEAL BEFORE A DATE AND THEN PICK AT YOUR FOOD LIKE A BIRD ON THE DATE.

DON'T ORDER A PUDDING – EAT YOUR BOYFRIEND'S.

JEANETTE ...ANKY DIET	THE VANESSA FELTZ DIET	THE LENA ZAVARONI DIET	THE TINKERBELL DIET	THE SINDY DIET
a genetic defect. ...rm an energetic ...act with your ...ly freaky husband.	Binge in secret, due to the pressure of having no talent for your job. Labour under the misapprehension that personality is enough and that you have one. Ugly weight gain. Film deal opposite Kermit the Frog.	Don't eat at all. Have pushy parent who coast on your success.	Be a fairy – they are not known for weight problems. Get all the children in the world to say they don't believe in fairies.	Be a plastic moulded doll.
...l never be heavy ...e a dwarf. Minor ...rity status on Border		Significant weight loss generally and total weight loss on TV, on which you are now invisible.	Significant light loss into total darkness. Children's tears.	Maintain your perfect figure and abnormally long legs. Have a boyfriend with no willy.

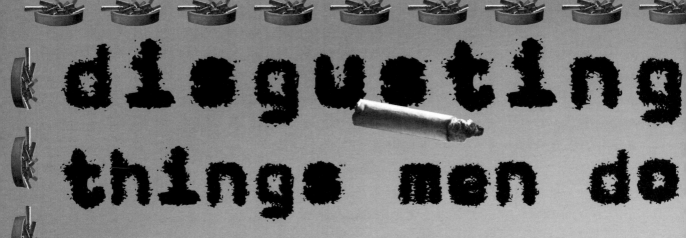

disgusting things men do

If we had to list all the disgusting things men do, it would probably fill enough books to keep the local library thriving for years. The sad thing is that many men reading the following list are likely to say, "Well, what's wrong with that?" It has simply never occurred to some poor, sad, backward Neanderthal that anything on this list is a totally gross thing to do.

Leaving stubble in the sink

How many times have you screamed with fright at what looks like a colony of ants in the sink, only to realise that, yet again, Samson has neglected to rinse away his chin clippings. Perhaps he does it to try and reassert his masculinity in the bathroom. After all, this is a place that does tend to get colonised by female frippery – five different kinds of shampoo, sanitary goods, collections of sea-shells. All the same, it's disgusting and extremely anti-social.

Allowing socks to become grow-bags

Though a man can seldom be trusted to keep a pot plant alive, he can always be relied upon to grow a good crop of bacteria in his discarded socks. These putrescent articles get so lively after a few weeks of lying around under the sofa,

or huddling together for warmth in old sports bags, that they can walk by themselves into the launderette. Or at least that's what men say, when you ask why they don't pick them up.

Making roll-ups from old nub-ends

The dedicated nicotine-head, after a hard night out scrounging everybody else's fags, will often find he has none of his own at home when he desperately craves the sixtieth snout of the day. Nothing for it but to scrape all those little blackened bits of tobacco out of the dog-ends in the overflowing ashtrays, and make a DIY ciggie that tastes like the bits of burnt stuff you find in the bottom of a grill-pan. (You know this because you made the mistake of kissing him afterwards.)

Which brings us to...

Abusing the grill-pan

Never accept grilled fish fingers from your bloke's kitchen. They will be smoked through by the flavour of five years of collected bacon fat and garnished with small lumps of dense black stuff, which 300 million years ago was probably toast.

Missing the toilet bowl

Why do men spray wee-wee on the floor around the lavatory? Is it that their penises, contrary to popular belief, do not have a single jet, but are fitted with a watering can attachment which sprinkles over a wide area? Is it that they are so busy making Robert de Niro in *Taxi Driver* faces in the

mirror that they cannot concentrate on the job in hand? Do they wilfully and deliberately aim their pee-sticks at the bathroom mat, in revenge at their mothers for buying them nasty girly pink things, like bathroom mats, for presents when they wanted beer and fags? Or are they just pigs?

Not cutting his toenails

You're flailing around with your man in a delicious orgy of mutual lust, sexily kitted out in some super-fine stockings, when he takes off his shoes and socks. Suddenly your legs are being ripped to shreds by Edward Scissorfeet. How some people find sticking a bloke's ragged horny toenails in their gob a turn-on is beyond rational explanation.

Expelling wind in inappropriate places

The diet of the male lends itself to intestinal fermentation: large quantities of yeast-filled items such as beer and bread, together with undigested red meat and fizz-filled energy-drinks, give him enough gas-producing capability to fuel the cookers of a medium-sized African country. Sadly, men don't tend to use this gas to improve the lot of developing nations, but instead choose to release it in delicate, or poignant, s i t u a t i o n s –

- when he first meets your mother
- in the quiet moment after the bride has said "I do"

- when he's just finished reading out a beautiful poem to you about how much he loves you
- when you've wrapped your arms around his thighs and are resting your head on his bottom.

Not washing their hands

Women tend to wash their hands after every activity that could be termed dirty. They also do a lot of washing up and hand-washing of delicate woollens, so their paws are always pristine. Men don't wash their hands unless they absolutely have to, for example when their fingers are so stuck together with bike oil that they can't hold a fag. To test the grubbiness of his fingers, take a good sniff of them now – have a sick-bag ready...

Snoring

The irritating thing is that you can't tell a snorer by appearances. The most cherubic, gorgeous, doe-eyed boy can turn into a grunting, honking grizzly bear when the sex is over and he's nodded off. If he's really adorable, you could stick it out with the help of earplugs and toler-ance. If not, punch him till he stops, or lock him in the car for the night.

Chatting up traffic wardens

There is nothing more repugnant than witnessing a bloke trying to get off a parking ticket by oozing all over a female traffic warden. All the old clichés come out: "I love a girl in uniform", "You're far too pretty to be doing this job", "Take back that ticket and I'll give you a night to remember". It's all the more pathetic because the warden is sneering so hard that her face is going to fall off. When at last, disgusted, she spits at his feet and walks off, he will inevitably say, "Tight-arsed bitch needs a good shagging", at which point you will hit him over the head with a piece of handy scaffolding.

First of all, there are a few vital points to remember if you are successfully to enter one of the last great bastions of machismo: football is a bloke's game, first, last and always. Don't be fooled by the occasional nod towards women supporters on *Fantasy Football League.* That's why it's called "Fantasy". As with the police force, the armed services and stand-up comedy, you are allowed in by law, but you are not welcome. Unlike sex, violence, religion and relationships, in which blokes will indulge when they feel it's necessary, football is the only outlet for honest emotion. Men will laugh and cry and hug each other with the abandon of children. This is very precious to them and should be mocked at every available opportunity. Football is a fabulous game. If you do find yourself becoming a fan, do not let on that you have any knowledge

whatsoever. In conversations about football, girls are only allowed to comment on Ryan Giggs's legs, David Ginola's Gallic beauty and Eric Cantona's turned-up collar (purely in terms of its fashion value). Football is a winter sport. It is most important, therefore, that when you are invited to "get your tits out for the lads", you decline (however tempting it might be), as you will probably catch a rather nasty chest cold.

On the Pull – On the Terraces ...

This is a hazardous journey to be undertaken only by the extremely brave or foolhardy. It involves preparations comparable to an arctic expedition.

WHAT SORT OF MEN TO EXPECT:
Apart from on the pitch, you are unlikely to find a French philosopher/poet at any football ground in Britain. If you fancy a bit of rough along the lines of West Ham hard man Julian Dicks (with a name like that you learn to be tough) then the terraces could be hog heaven for you.

THE STRONG SILENT TYPE
This man takes his football very seriously indeed. He hasn't missed a match home or away since 1978, and that was only because he had to have a kidney removed. He never joins in the chanting, as he considers that is for part-timers. He never speaks or reacts, it is almost as if he thinks he is controlling the game through sheer force of will. There is absolutely no chance of getting off with him unless you are his team captain's sister, mum or granny.

THE COMMENTATOR
This is the guy who seems to think that nobody else in the stands can actually see the game, so he feels the need to give it the full John Motson for ninety minutes. Intensely irritating, but if you are interested you'll have to be quite quick, because he is liable to get a slap (particularly from "strong & silent").

THE JOKER
With a group of mates who don't really like him very much, but he's allowed to go with them because he drives them all to away matches. He thinks it's incredibly funny to taunt the players with comments about their private lives from last week's *News of the World* e.g. "Does your missus know you're here?"

WHAT TO WEAR
Football grounds are not the most hospitable places in the world. Although many of us are prepared to sacrifice comfort for style, in this case it would be a little extreme. You wouldn't wear your best clothes to visit a public toilet, and we are talking about a very similar venue here. Once again, the football season is in the winter, so do wrap up. However, football supporters do like their girls to look like girls. So while it is best to avoid mini-skirts and boob-tubes, do try to be quite pink and fluffy, with maybe some ribbons and shiny jewellery.

Do not under any circumstances wear the team strip – there is nothing more naff. This is actually one of the few equal opportunity rules, as it also applies to the boys.

WHAT TO DO
Despite the intellectualisation of football by the likes of Nick Hornby and Skinner & Baddiel, this is not New Man territory, so you may have to be a little cunning. If you have avoided actually having blonde highlights and surgically attached stiletto heels, then you will just have to act dumb.

Don't talk during the actual game. Make your move at half-time and ask him who is winning. This will achieve two objectives, getting him to talk about what he loves and immediately showing your interest and ignorance.

Make sure you ask what offside means at least twice just to make sure. If you do manage to score and you are not totally repulsed by your trophy, you may find a football supporter quite handy as a boyfriend. Due to the current busy league schedule he will be unavailable two, or maybe three, times a week including cup matches. This means you have loads of free time without having to make excuses. Also, he will be so preoccupied, particularly during championship or relegation battles, that you will have no trouble shagging around behind his back.

However, you might just fall in love with the football instead of the boys, go to matches with your mates, learn important phrases such as "Come on ref, he took the ball/his legs/a dive, where's your white stick?" And if you do get asked out by a loyal supporter, just tell him you'd rather be blowing bubbles.

WHAT NOT TO DO

 Throw your knickers at Ryan Giggs just as he shoots at goal. He might miss.

Throw your knickers at Gazza just as he shoots at goal. He might put them on his head.

 Shout "Get your cock out for the girls". Somebody just might.

Hit a policeman – they hit back.

Try to start a Mexican wave – nobody will follow and you will look a fool.

Shout "What a shot by Shearer!" when it was Asprilla.

 Request the DJ to play "Oops Upside Your Head" at half-time and then do the dance.

Ask the bloke next to you to save your space while you go to the loo.

Eat the pies. 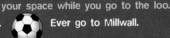 Ever go to Millwall.

GREAT *Girl*

I'M ONLY STRINGING HIM ALONG!

Dream On

SAME T-SHIRT DIFFERENT DAY

See insid for Personalit

T-SHIRTS

Virgin

I'VE GOT MY PERIOD SO I MAY BE UNREASONABLE

Lian

TOO SOBER TO FUCK

My other boyfriend's a girlfriend

BUY ME A CAR
And I'll show you my tits!

A dog is man's best friend, but the telephone is most definitely woman's best friend. What on earth did women do before phones were invented? Well, they had to train to try and communicate through the air with their distant female friends – hence the development of female intuition and the large number of witches, soothsayers and wise women before the invention of the phone. Of course, we all know that it was Mrs Bell who told Alexander Graham to build her idea for a phone, so that she could call her best friend Prudence who lived across town.

Since then, women worldwide have spent at least five hours a day on the phone, purely socially, and never exhibit any surprise at the obscenely high bills.

Phone technology advances daily, as women quest for the ideal phone. Phone companies and switchboards have a very high percentage of female staff, who all strive towards this goal. Here is a prototype for that dream phone.

Things to Say to Dirty Callers

"Oh great, I'm so glad you called, I'll just switch on the tape recorder."

"Hello, this is PC Weatherspoon."

"Spam, Spam, Spam, Spam, do you know where I can get some Spam? Do you have any? Do you like it? I mean, do you really like it? What do you most like about it? Do you ever wear it for its decorative properties...?"

VERY LOUD BELL

CALLER DISPLAY INFORMATION

EMERY BOARD

EXTENDABLE LEAD FOR REACHING ALL AREAS OF THE HOUSE, INCLUDING THE LOO, AND ACROSS TO THE CORNER SHOP

The ideal girl's phone should have certain numbers automatically programmed into it:

1. Phone tarot
2. Pizza delivery
3. Ex-boyfriend's new girlfriend
4. The Samaritans
5. Alcoholics Anonymous

VOICE DISGUISING OPTIONS
- **HUNKY MAN**
- **NON-ENGLISH SPEAKING**
- **DALEK**
- **PINKY AND PERKY**
- **STEPHEN HAWKING**

ROSE TINTED SCRAMBLER FOR AUTOMATIC EDITING OF ANYTHING YOU DON'T WANT TO HEAR

CHOCOHOLICS ANONYMOUS

EARPIECE STUN FACILITY

SLAM BUTTON FOR EXTRA LOUD SLAM

TOTALLY WATERPROOF FOR IMMERSION IN THE BATH

SOFT FOAM HANDSET FOR LYING ON OR USING AS AN ALICE BAND

AUTOMATIC BLOCK ON CALLS
FROM: BANK MANAGER
SURVEY PEOPLE
MOTHER AFTER ONE HOUR
TO: EX-BOYFRIEND AFTER 50 CALLS IN 24 HOURS

VANITY MIRROR

BOTTLE OPENER

FAG LIGHTER

TISSUES

Messages to put on your answerphone

1. "I've only gone out for 3 minutes 40 seconds, so please, please, please leave a message or ring straight back after that time has elapsed."

2. "I'm away for a week, but I've left a wolf in the flat."

3. "The whole of the Country & Western song 'I'll be over you when the grass is over me'."

4. "I may be in, but I loathe humanity too much to pick up the phone and I'll make sarky comments out loud while I screen your call."

5. "I'm sorry I'm not in. Please leave a message after the tone... And if that's *you* – I hope you suffer a slow and painful death, you've ruined my life."

INSTANT LINE CHECK FOR FAULTS – TO SAVE GETTING A FRIEND TO RING YOU

SPECIAL LIGHT THAT DENOTES IT'S HIM

TURNS KETTLE ON

FIVE POSSIBLE LATE-NIGHT, DEAD-CERT SHAGS

PRESS TO INTERRUPT ENGAGED SIGNAL

TRACKING DEVICE – ESPECIALLY FOR 1471 DENIED NUMBERS

GIRLS
on Holiday

Barring childbirth, bereavement, and the sudden mid-rave realisation that your Dayglo mini-dress is firmly lodged inside your Asda pants – going on holiday is probably the most traumatic experience of a girl's life. Before you leave, you'll need jabs against diseases like malaria, dysentery, cholera, yellow fever, beri-beri and swamp foot. If you're going further than Blackpool you might need even more. These are important, so don't wimp out. Just imagine the whole business as being like bad sex. A little prick, over in seconds – and at least when the Doc asks you to swallow, the sugar lump does taste quite nice.

IMPORTANT THINGS TO PACK

✓ Condoms

✓ Good supply of Danielle Steel novels (to counter embarrassing hotel bathroom bog-roll crisis)

✓ Passport

✓ Sunglasses (so no-one recognises you as the goofy Nana Mouskouri look-alike in your passport photo)

✓ Paper bags (in case of travel sickness, or waking up with a hangover and particularly ugly bedfellow)

✓ Bilingual edition of 101 Chat-Up Lines for Girls

✓ Super-Size Pantie Pads with Special Lockaway Core (can double as handy hotel-room draught excluder)

✓ Sexy undies (for pulling)

✓ Normal undies (for paranoid flyers, worried that the emergency parachute will fail to open).

IMPORTANT THINGS NOT TO PACK

✗ Boyfriend

✗ Femidoms (too much hassle having to check each one in separately at airport baggage control).

There are two types of holiday – the British holiday, and the good holiday. Key factors to bear in mind, when deciding whether to abandon our native climes for somewhere more exotic.

CONTINENTAL HOLIDAY

☀ Beach bums remind you of guys on TV's Baywatch

☀ Hotel has large warm indoor pool

☀ Can shag hunky Italian bloke without having to understand a word he's saying

☀ Chance to experience foreign cultures

☀ Skin goes brown quickly on beach

☀ Crappy discos full of pallid lads from Stockport

☀ Lots of bad dancing to "Saturday Night" by Whigfield

BRITISH HOLIDAY

💧 Beach bums remind you of guys on TV's Crimewatch

💧 Hotel *loo* has large indoor pool

💧 Can shag ugly Scouse bloke without having to understand a word he's saying

💧 Chance to experience foreign cultures growing on takeaway kebab

💧 Skin goes brown very quickly on beach (see: British beaches, pollution, problem of)

💧 Crappy discos full of pallid lads from Stockport

💧 Lots of bad dancing to "Saturday Night" by Whigfield

Holidays are an opportunity for today's hard-working career girl to relax, combat executive stress, broaden her cultural perspectives and, most importantly, pull someone who isn't British and might therefore be OK in the sack. Top tip for any girls trying Sex Sans Frontières, though – national bonking techniques have much in common with national cooking techniques...

ITALIAN *(Pizza)*: Will argue for ages to get what he wants on top. But does offer choice between eat-in or take-out

FRENCH *(Garlic mushrooms)*: Best have some strong mints handy for afterwards

ORIENTAL *(Crispy prawn balls)*: Disappointing small portions. Only satisfies one person. Will leave you wanting more 20 minutes later

AMERICAN *(Burger)*: Big hunk of beefcake, nicely packaged buns, sadly guaranteed to come in 30 seconds flat. Have a nice day now!

GREEK *(Moussaka – traditional farmhouse fayre)*: Hung like a donkey, equally stubborn. May disconcertingly want it "just like Mama used to do"

BRITISH *(Yorkshire pud)*: Pale, fatty, often reluctant to rise

DANISH *(Bacon)*: Streaky back. Exercise caution – possibly an S & M freak.

Don't expect too much from your continental conquests. Remember, it's not a proper holiday unless at least one of the party ends up going down with something (or on someone) unpleasant.

There is one major difference between men and women drivers – women have two hands on the steering wheel, whereas men only use one. Why do you think this is? This is not to say that women are cissy drivers. Far from it! Driving a car is like being with a man – treat it nicely and you can get it to do anything you want.

BEING A FEMALE DRIVER HAS MANY ADVANTAGES...

Breaking Down

You must always remember to carry two things with you in the car in case of a breakdown. They are a Wonderbra and a bottle of peroxide. If you look like a dumb blonde with the potential to shag like a bunny, you will have no trouble getting unsuspecting men to stop and fix your distributor cap. Again, giggling is the key here, preferably with your mouth open. Once the car has been fixed and is ready to go, tell him you're very grateful, but you have to pick your girlfriend up on the way to a KD Lang concert.

Being Stopped by the Police for Speeding

If you are stopped by a WPC, this is slightly tricky. Try to bond on a sisterly level by telling her that you've just caught your boyfriend in bed with your best friend. Then start crying. Not a sniffle, but real full-blown snotty cry. That should do the trick. If you're stopped by a man, then you're laughing. The best way to get out of a speeding ticket is to inform the officer that you've got a raging case of cystitis, and if you don't get to a toilet immediately, you're going to piss all over the seat. This should create a few moments of nervous stammering, followed by a warning not to do it again, which of course you solemnly swear to adhere to.

Passing Your Test

Make sure you do this as soon as you are seventeen, before your legs know the meaning of cellulite. Find the shortest skirt and the lowest top possible, and off you go for a sure first-time pass (unless you have a female examiner, then you're up shit street without a roundabout). Every time you change gear, rub the examiner's thigh with your hand, just like your instructor taught you to. If you do make a complete hash of it, you can always giggle a lot and offer him a blow-job (for emergencies only)

GIRLS &

Common Girlie Mistakes

Depressing the Clutch
This does not mean constantly playing Leonard Cohen tapes in the car

Alarming your Car
This does not involve telling your car that you're about to scrap it.

Buying a Car
When purchasing a car you may want to haggle with the dealer and ask him to go down. He may be willing to do this, but it may cost you more in the end.

Your Big End
A mechanic may at some stage tell you that your big end has gone. This is not a compliment.

Girlie Translation of Mechanic-Speak:

"IT'LL BE READY ON TUESDAY"

"WE'LL SEE WHAT WE CAN DO BEFORE 2PM"

"We're closed on Tuesday, you'll be lucky if you get it before Christmas"

"We'll sit on our arses till 1.55pm, then tell you it'll need a closer look"

"IT'LL COST YOU"

"IT'S ONLY A SCRATCH, LOVE"

"It'll cost you"

"You'll need a whole new body panel and respray"

A GIRL'S GUIDE TO The Highway Code

 Wonderbras must be worn

 Cross your heart only

 As if!

 Caution. Femidom factory

 Red and black cars only

 Shagfest ahead (Humps for 1 mile)

 Little Chef ahead.

DRIVING

The Perfect Man

It's hard to let go of the dream of The Perfect Man. No matter how often men let us down, we still persist in believing that somewhere there exists a wonderful piece of man flesh who is sublime in every way and who will love us forever and ever, unconditionally (even when we've got cellulite from our knees to our necks). Let's have a look at our expectations and the grim realities.

ADORATION

You may receive a whole lot of this in the first two months of seduction. As soon as he thinks he's got you, however, he'll start treating you like a nice old beanbag he can lean against when he's watching videos.

COMMITMENT

A word guaranteed to strike fear into the heart of all boyfriends. Most chaps would rather cut off their own legs than pledge to stay with a woman forever. If you do get him to say "till death us do part", check out his fingers – they'll be crossed. The only men who want to be committed are those who should be.

GREAT SEX

The definition of this varies widely. Suffice it to say that if you're the kind of girl who likes red-hot rumpy-pumpy action all night long, you will tend to attract impotent blokes who would rather have a cuddle. On the other hand, if you want gentle caressing, your men will be wham-bam brutes whose only aim in sex is to release some pressure in their testicles.

DROP-DEAD GORGEOUSNESS

If he's too handsome, he'll be constantly pursued by lusty women, some of whom will be better-looking than you. If he's too pretty, he'll be constantly pursued by lusty men...some of whom will be better-looking than you.

What Girls Want & What Girls Get

INTELLIGENCE

Men can be clever, but only about certain subjects, like footballing heroes of the '60s or state-of-the-art software packages. When it comes to anything useful, like psychology, organisation or how to make fairy cakes, women are leagues ahead.

A NEAT LITTLE BOTTOM

What looks quite good in jeans can be a pimply, hairy, flabby thing when the pants are down – unless he works out, in which case the muscles are so tight, you can't get a grip.

A GOOD SENSE OF HUMOUR

A man who can have a really good laugh, but only at his own jokes, *Viz* magazine or Vic & Bob, and never at your pithy little anecdotes.

DOMESTICITY

Even if a bloke doesn't live like a swamp thing from the bog, he can only ever manage selected household tasks. Men often take responsibility for one job only, such as putting in window locks, and then claim they've made their contribution.

PLENTY OF MONEY

Of course, these days girls don't want to be kept women, but a stash of dosh does help. Sadly, rich men are either mad, mean or megalomaniac, and you will be less important to him than his balance sheets.

ABSENCE OF NEUROSES

Here are just a few common mental problems in men: obsessive disorders, mother-fixations, alcoholism, infantilism, hypochondria, fetishism, competitiveness, workaholism, homicidal mania, competitiveness, rage and loss of male pride due to going bald. Your average man will have at least three of these.

This might all seem rather bleak, but if you're prepared to compromise like mad, put up with some appalling behaviour and lower your expectations to almost nothing, you can still find a man to call your own. If you do give up the quest for The Perfect Man, you can always just use blokes for the odd night and spend much more quality time with the girls. Sorted.

The GETTING READY TO GO OUT Routine

This is a girl's favourite ritual, an essential process whereby she transforms herself from a lumpy greaseball in leggings into a glorious, sparkling, foxy vamp. Three hours minimum should be allowed, and special girlfriends may be invited to join in.

DO CHECK-LIST

Stockings un-laddered?

Bra loaded correctly?

Any stray hairs on black clothing?

Any cack on shoes?

Lipstick on teeth?

Condoms in purse
(if you're feeling lucky).

First, chill your wine — a glass of Marks & Sparks Soave will provide vital energy for the night ahead.

Run the bath — add half the contents of the Body Shop.

Put on a CD compilation of dance music and turn up to ear-cracking volume. Shave legs, pits and bikini line (if you're feeling lucky).

Wash hair, condition it, towel dry, add post-conditioning conditioner and comb-through mousse, blow dry, spray on curl enhancer, tweak, cover in hairspray, brush half of it out, add ribbons, grips, bobbles, etc.

Get in bath. Loofah, pumice, scrub, exfoliate and massage.

Smooth body oil over all the bits of flesh that are going to show.

Ring your girlfriend and check what she's wearing so that you don't clash.

Pour wine. Look at contents of wardrobe. Realise you're too fat for half of it and the other half's gone out of fashion. Throw yourself on the bed weeping.

Paint nails. Jog round the dog while they dry. Eat some yogurt to line your stomach.

Dress slowly, looking at yourself in the mirror as you add each new item. Do your "I am a beautiful woman" affirmations ten times.

Remember — there's no body that a Wonderbra and a pair of five-inch wedges can't fix. Put on some decent knickers if you feel lucky.

THE MAKE-UP: best done slowly, using three different mirrors and with a fabulous selection of cosmetics, ranging from a bit of dried-up eyeliner you've had since 1983 to a state-of-the-art lip pencil that cost more than your car. If you haven't done it, don't go in for eyebrow plucking or moustache-bleaching at this stage, or your face will look like a pizza.

Choose handbag (allow fifteen minutes for this — accessories can make or break an outfit). Set the video for _Friends._

Ring up your girlfriend and tell her you'll be late. Put perfume on neck, wrists, cleavage, backs of knees and anywhere else you can think of.

IF ALL'S IN ORDER, trip out to the mini-cab office, more carefully than usual on account of the heels, and plaster a big saucy Come-and-talk-to-me smile on your face. Women are going to gasp in admiration and men will besiege you with compliments and offers of marriage. Well, they better had, because God knows, you don't get any better than this ...

GIRLS' NIGHT OUT

We've all been on the girls' night out. Some end in tears, others in casualty, but the next day you ring your mates and swear that, although you're never going to drink again, it was the best night out in ages. And it was. By girls' night out we don't mean a couple of you hitting the pub straight from work – we mean business. It's when a bunch of mates decide to get

5 pm

From work to your mate's house to get ready, drink vodka and apply mascara in time to Pulp. A necessary part of this process is the **swap**. Something from her wardrobe catches your eye – normally you wouldn't clean your windows with it, but tonight it will make you look like Uma Thurman in *Pulp Fiction*. The vodka has started working.

7.30 pm

"The Addams Family" try to hail a cab. Finally you get one to stop and it's off to the wine bar. It's crowded and full of blokes who think you must be on the pull. Normally pint-drinkers, you and your mate decide that tonight is tequila night – it gets you high and you're feeling exotic. Oh dear, toilets all over the city are bracing themselves. So the night is officially started, but where to go?

together (one or two of those scheduled to come won't have been out with the gals for ages) and have an event: drinking, dancing and telling really dirty true stories that mean you'll never look each other's lovers in the face again. "He asked you to do what? With a biro?"

Crap Discos

How does this happen? Why is it that whenever you walk into a sleazy neon-lit disco playing '80s music there's only ever a group of fairly oiled-looking women and a couple of sad lonely men in *Brookside* perms? Sad, because they suspect they're getting nowhere with the girls on the town, which is confirmed when the "ladies" leap up to dance to "Like a Virgin" in only their bras. The men may as well go home. "Like a Virgin" is a girl thing. If you ever get to a decent club you can guarantee it is only because one of your number is sober (driving) and said NO to "Raquel's" on the High Street. It doesn't matter that they're doing cheap Martini. It's a bad idea.

Comedy Clubs

A lot of comedy clubs no longer allow Stag Nights, because of the bad behaviour. There's nothing a comedian hates more than a bunch of pissed-up blokes heckling the stage. Well, there is one thing: a bunch of girls. They're trouble, because they know that they're loads funnier than the guy on stage talking about what he does when he's watching *Baywatch* (yawn), or about the time his mum caught him doing *it*. But very foolish is the male comedian who tells "my girlfriend is so stupid/ugly/fat" jokes (in a post-feminist ironic manner, of course, dear). Men have been seen heckled into submission by bloodlust Hen Parties shouting "Get your knob out" in a very non-ironic threatening tone. From that first realisation and the loud stage whisper "He's a bit crap, isn't he?", mob rule quickly grows. He got his knob out, and it was the biggest laugh of the night.

Restaurants

It starts with "Let's go for a quiet meal, we can talk and drink and harass the male waiters". That's how it starts, but somehow cocktails enter the equation and it becomes that salsa lambada bar that does bar snacks. A great success, apart from the badly bruised area you get from being whisked around the dance floor by a lambada stallion brandishing an erection he's trying very hard to insert through your pubic bone.

The Way Home

Remember, girls being drunk and mouthy don't usually get punched – it's the guy standing nearest to them that generally cops it (worth remembering the next time your beloved pisses you off in public – just insult the nearest gorilla and wait). Girls do, however, get arrested. Telling the guy who is closing the gate at the Tube what you think of the travel system in London is not the best idea. You knew all that when you left the house, and it's the quickest way to a night in a cell. Buying chips and staggering into a cab is the more favoured option, then crying all the way home as you tell him your life story.

The Next Morning

You feel fantastic (apart from the head) and phone Karen. "When do we do it again...? Tonight?"

Blind date

Sometimes the most wonderful thing to be is a single girl. You have nobody to answer to or consider. What a joy it is to eat toast in bed and not worry about the crumbs. Listen to Boyzone when you want, watch *Knots Landing* when there is sport on (not because you want to, but because you can).

Unfortunately, there always comes a time when your friends have to spoil it for you. Friends who are in relationships always assume that you must be miserable because you are not. The fact that you spend much of your day every day listening to them talk about all their problems with their boyfriends, while you are having a fab time, does not stop them from feeling sorry for you because you don't have what they have.

Eventually, after dropping hints and then openly trying to make you feel inadequate, they start trying to set you up with people. You know the story: "My Barry's got this friend at work who has just split up with his girlfriend; he's a real laugh. Barry reckons the four of us should go out one night."

Now you know you are about to enter the seventh circle of hell. But it's only a night out, what harm could it do...?

THE FRIEND OF A FRIEND (TYPE 1)

So your best mate's boyfriend has got a mate at work. Apparently he is very successful: great car, lovely house and has recently become single. What they omit to tell you is the reason he recently single. He has the personality of a walnut, with a penis to match. He's got a great car and a great home because he does nothing but work, and on the rare occasions that he isn't actually working, he is talking about it. Now, for some people quantity surveying may be riveting, but most of us will find ourselves asking questions like, "So these quantities, quite large, are they?", then drinking our own body weight in wine at dinner, and the last thing you'll remember will be giggling, "What was that? Quorn titty surfing?", before falling into a coma.

THE FRIEND OF A FRIEND (TYPE 2)

OK, why not? So this time your friend tells you that she's got this best friend since school who is the loveliest guy in the world, and she just knows that you will hit it off. You are starting to think this might be all right and then she uses the phrase which is designed to strike fear into the heart of even the strongest of women – "He's got a lovely personality" – and that is when you know with horrifying certainty that he looks like the creature from the black lagoon. If only he was that good-looking. You spend an evening with a nice, nice man, but it's difficult to hear what he's actually saying above the sniggers of the waiting staff and people at the next table speculating as to whether you are out with him for a bet.

BLIND DATE

Things are getting very desperate now. So yes, you are actually going to go on *Blind Date*. The first decision you have to make as a *Blind Date* contestant is whether you are going to be the pretty, deliberately obtuse one, the aloof educated one or the loud wacky one. You know in your heart that it doesn't matter, as the level of humiliation will be numbing to the point of excluding any real consciousness. The questions you will be asked will be along the lines of: "What flower are you most like?" or "Where would you most like to go on holiday?" In translation: "Will you give me a blow job, even if we miss the holiday in Tahiti and end up pot-holing in Somerset?" If you give the right answers you might get chosen by the law student from Surrey, who is only there because his mates set him up. You will hate each other and then have to endure Cilla asking you whether she should buy a new hat.

LONELY HEARTS AD

You have been happily single for about six months, but your friend has got to you and you are now completely paranoid. So what's wrong with me? Why haven't I got a boyfriend? You then find yourself idly scanning the lonely hearts columns for a laugh. One bad day, you're on your own, a bit pissed, a bit pre-menstrual – so you decide to answer one. You justify it by thinking: Well, they can't all be sad freaks, because after all I'm reading it and I'm fabulous. So you end up replying to: "Successful business man, own penthouse apartment and yacht, handsome thirtysomething, seeks strong adventurous younger woman for endless fun". You arrange to meet. A bit suspicious when the designated point is La Hore kebab house in the East End of London. Still, he might be an eccentric millionaire. His successful business turns out to be a handbag stall on Petticoat Lane market, and his penthouse apartment turns out to be a bedsit on the Mile End Road. However, he's got a boat, but sadly a leaky speedboat about as big as your average bathtub, moored on the Manchester Ship Canal. Thirtysomething turns out to be forty-six. He is looking for a strong woman to help him bail out the water in the boat and shift the gear on his stall. Adventurous means that he is hoping you would urinate on him in the bath on the first date, which he tells you before you've finished your first Malibu and Coke – (his choice, 'cos you look like a bit of class, apparently). To add insult to injury, he is as disappointed as you are, because when he said younger woman he was hoping for sixteen, maybe seventeen ("all legal and above board, you understand, although I don't mind if they look younger").

The REAL Blind Date

Obviously if your date is actually blind, you don't have to worry about shaving under your arms or the possible pitfalls of a bad eyeliner day...

nightclubb

When Stone Age Man and Stone Age Woman used to go out for a "hard night's clubbing", they would return covered in sweat and grime, lugging the bloodied carcasses of various small furry animals whose skulls they'd smashed. Modern clubbing is far less civilised. No street-sassy girlie would be seen dead in a loincloth (except, perhaps, one made of shocking pink fur fabric with a silver trim). If you're going to be a serious club babe, you want something far more revealing.

Drugs

If you go to a nightclub, you may be tempted to take drugs. **Do not do this**: pay for them like everyone else does. Because we are all socially responsible, here's a handy reference guide to some dangerous substances you may be offered.

Stimulants

Examples	Speed, "Whizz"
On the up side	Will make you dance like Michael Jackson
On the down side	Will make you dance like Michael Jackson

Depressants

Examples	Like I really can't be bothered to list them all, y' know?
Uppers	Will stop you dancing like Michael Jackson
Downers	Can induce dangerous side-effects, such as a desire to consume Pot Noodles and copious quantities of Dunkin' Donuts at 5.30am.

Hallucinogens

Examples	LSD, Acid
Uppers	May make your date metamorphose into purple elephants. Definite bonus if he's not particularly "well-hung."
Downers	Chance of experiencing a "bad trip", i.e. a bus ride to Oxfam to purchase embarrassing-type gear. Inexplicable craving to christen your offspring Aurora and Moonblossom, which they probably won't appreciate at Newcastle Boys Grammar.

ng

Clubber Clobber

When going to a particular club for the first time, remember that the right gear is vitally important. Every club has its own individual and bizarre dress-code. This is a social minefield, which would have lesser women yearning wistfully for the tarty simplicity of the dreaded sixth-form disco. Fortunately, we are made of sterner stuff. We know there's a sure way to suss out the dress-code of any club. Whatever you're wearing when you turn up at the door, that's **not** it.

But there's no need to get your knickers in a twist (unless you're planning to strut your funky stuff at "Twisted Pan Night" every other Friday with DJ Lucy L Astik). Like your average bouncer, rectifying the problem is unbelievably simple. Just scarper to the nearest public bogs and swap clothes with your date. If he already happens to be wearing a metallic-look silver mini-skirt, all the better.

Only in very occasional cases will you also need to add a few tasteful accessories, for example two traffic cones stuffed inside the Wonderbra, or swaddle your entire torso in air-cushioned plastic packing wrap.

One note of advice, though. If you're going to a club that favours Seventies gear, try purple velvet hipsters, a clashing satin shirt and enough silver eye make-up to make you look like R2D2's big sister. (Seventies gear does not include a tartan shopping trolley, beige cardie, duffle coat that smells of piss and a colostomy bag. Not even if it's a designer colostomy bag.)

CHAT-UP LINES

You've been at the party for an hour, and at last you've spotted someone you might like. Before moving in with your best line, please check off the following:

☐ Are you sure, or are you desperate?

☐ Check out his jeans (are they Levis or Wranglers?) If Wrangler, see footnote*.

☐ Does he speak English?

☐ Is he snogging another woman? If so, see footnote**.

☐ Is he conscious? Remember, some men sleep standing up.

If you are happy with at least three of your answers, please go to Part II.

If you are not happy with at least three of your answers, see previous footnote.

PART II
N.B. REMEMBER, ALWAYS: MIRROR, SIGNAL, MANOEUVRE

I think I fancy you, but I'm not sure – can we chat for ten minutes, then I'll let you know.

I say, old chap, d'ya fancy a bit of rumpy-pumpy? (strictly posh people only)

Hello, my name is ... and I can lift my leg around my ear. (N.B. not recommended for pensioners out on the pull at the over-55's club)

That's a nice tie – can I sniff it?

* Are you prepared to give it a go?
** Are you absolutely sure you are prepared to give it a go?

2
THE SUPERMODEL
DASH OF WHITE WINE
TOP UP WITH SPARKLING
MINERAL WATER

**GARNISH WITH NOTHING,
SERVE WITH NOTHING, THINK
OF NOTHING AND WEAR NEXT
TO NOTHING.**

1
THE SHAZZA
1 SHOT RUM
2 SHOTS VODKA
1 SHOT TIA MARIA
4 SHOTS BABYCHAM
2 SHOTS ADVOCAAT
2 SHOTS MALIBU
DASH OF LAGER

**GARNISH WITHOUT A
CHERRY 'COS SHE'S
ALREADY LOST IT AND
SERVE WITH A HANDBAG
AND PAIR OF
WHITE STILETTOS.**

A Girl's Favourite Co

3

THE MILITANT DYKE

*10 PINTS SCRUMPY EXTERMINATOR
PECULIAR (DOWNED IN ONE)*

**GARNISH WITH DM'S AND
SERVE WITH A LARGE BAG
OF CHIPS ON THE SHOULDER.**

4

THE BLONDE

AS "SHAZZA" SANS LAGER.

**GARNISH WITH A GIGGLE
AND SERVE WITHOUT
PEROXIDE 'COS IT'S
NATURAL.**

5

THE CATHOLIC

*1 BOTTLE RED WINE
SEVERAL DOUBLE WHISKIES
HOLY WATER*

**GARNISH WITH GUILT AND
SERVE WITH PARANOIA.**

cKtaiL list

Most Embarrassing

Drunken Deeds

SOME MEN SAY that there is nothing more disgusting than a drunk woman. Obviously the sight of a pissed bloke outside the pub regurgitating thirty-two pints of lager and a vindaloo is a thing of beauty to behold. Drunken women have just as much right to throw up in public because at least they have the decency to be embarrassed afterwards

Pissed and perched on a bar stool, lighting up a tampon, then five minutes later pissed in the lavvy trying to insert a cigarette.

Hailing a police car instead of a taxi, and when you eventually manage to hail a taxi forgetting where you live, falling in and propositioning the driver when you realise you haven't got any money.

Propositioning your boss at the Christmas party, getting rejected and ending up getting off with the mail boy.

Telling your best friend the truth.

Bursting into tears for no obvious reason.

Losing your key and ringing the doorbell of every other flat but your own.

Having sex in a photo booth, then forgetting to collect the photos.

Phoning your ex in the middle of the night and declaring absolute love, only to hear a woman's voice at the other end.

Taking advantage of your pathetic state to experiment with bisexuality.

Trying to apply make-up in brightly lit toilets, only to emerge looking like a pantomime dame.

Staging an impromptu striptease.

BOYS

AS A GIRL gets a little older, and more experienced in the ways of men, she often finds that chaps of her own age or older come with a whole package of problems that she just can't be dealing with in her busy, independent lifestyle. But she still wants a bonk, and a bit of male company now and again. What better solution than the toy boy?

WHERE TO FIND THEM

Schools, youth clubs, scout camps. Hanging out with your little brother in the tree-house. At Oasis gigs. In your local squat (only young people can bear having no comforts). In the Dole office. Behind the counter at McDonalds on a Saturday morning. At pubs advertising "Beer – a pound a pint". In police cells, having been arrested for being young and a bloke. Trying out, but not buying, all the latest equipment in a hi-fi shop. In amusement arcades. Strawberry picking in the summer holidays. Amongst the sons of your older female friends.

HOW TO SEDUCE ONE

Compliment him on his goatee (a little patch of bum-fluff on his chin, all the beard he can grow, but he thinks it makes him look cool and dangerous). Start a conversation on the relative merits of makes of trainers. Ask him to come round and show you how to use your new computer (but don't let him play games on it, or he won't look at you again). Get him horribly drunk on a pint and a half of lager. Buy him the full set of *Power Rangers*.

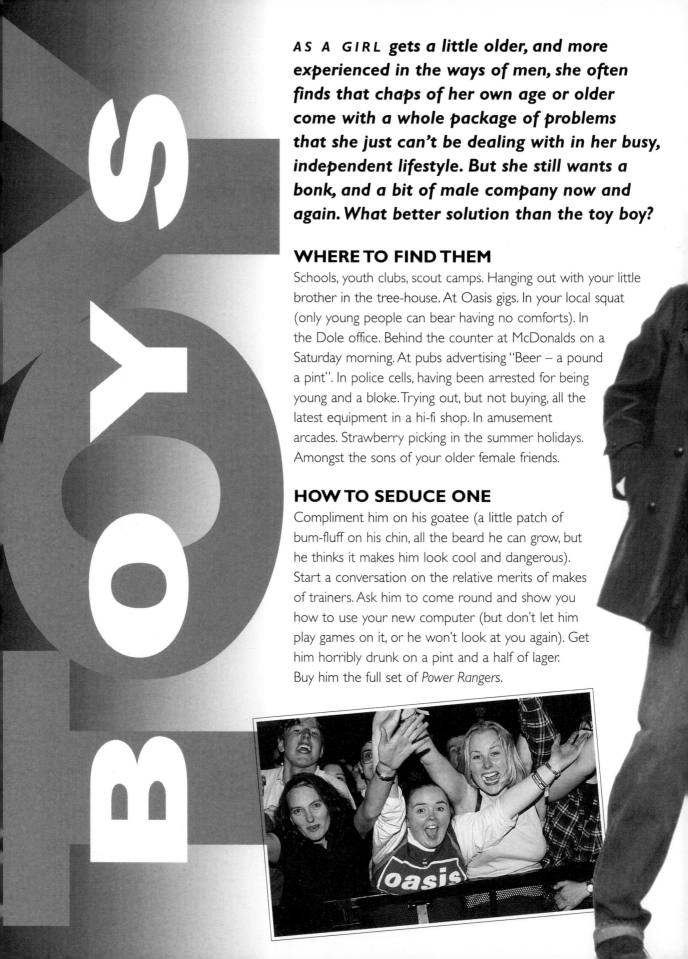

HOW TO KEEP ONE

Treat him like a puppy. Never refer to him in company as a boy, always as a man. Give him an ice-cream every time he gives you an orgasm. Keep acting the suave, sophisticated woman of the world – your power fascinates him. Give him pocket money. Don't get too fond of him.

ADVANTAGES OF A BOY LOVER

It's an ego boost: you must still be hot stuff if such a pretty young thing fancies you. He can keep it up all night (with short rests between spurts). He's less likely than an older man to want to move in on your space and take over your life (or make you a doormat, or a breeder, or a trophy-wife, or his cook and cleaner). He hasn't been so jaded by life's setbacks that he's lost his optimism (a toy-boy still believes in the possibility of world peace). His body is firm and taut, with no lumpy bits, pot-belly or hairy back. He's easily pleased (and cheap): give him a bag of chips and a can of pop and he's your slave for the night.

DISADVANTAGES OF A BOY LOVER

When you're out together, you feel like his mum. Conversation is limited: he hasn't done much, thought much or learned the art of witty banter. He hasn't got any money, so unless you pay for the lot, you aren't going to be popping over to Paris for dirty weekends on the Champs-Elysées. His friends (whom you don't fancy) seem like a bunch of gauche, crude adolescents whom you'd normally cross the road to avoid. His fresh, glowing body can make yours feel like a saggy, leathery, old bag. When you refer to bands/TV shows/fashions that you liked in your youth, he doesn't know what you're talking about. There is the nagging feeling that while you're spending time with him, you might be missing a decent older man who could be a better bet in the long term... .

The Female CONDO

The female condom (or Femidom) could only have been invented by a man, in revenge for having constantly to squash his precious package into the unsightly male condom for all these years. After all, it's not as if women have had to sort out any other contraception of their own before (unless you count the cap, the pill, the IUD, the coil and the oh so successful sponge, that is).

As if we want to clad our vaginal walls with rubber ... er... no thanks.

Still, the family planning department thought it would be a good idea to give us truckfuls of the buggers, so here's a few other things that you can do with the fabulous female condom:

1 The obvious one to start with is, of course, the carrier bag, but we think they make much better bin-liners. After all, most female condoms are used to handling rubbish.

2 Stupidly agreed to go camping but forgot to take something with you to keep you warm at night? No need to worry when you've got "Friendly Femmy, the 22-tog sleeping bag". It will keep you hot and cosy, whatever the weather.

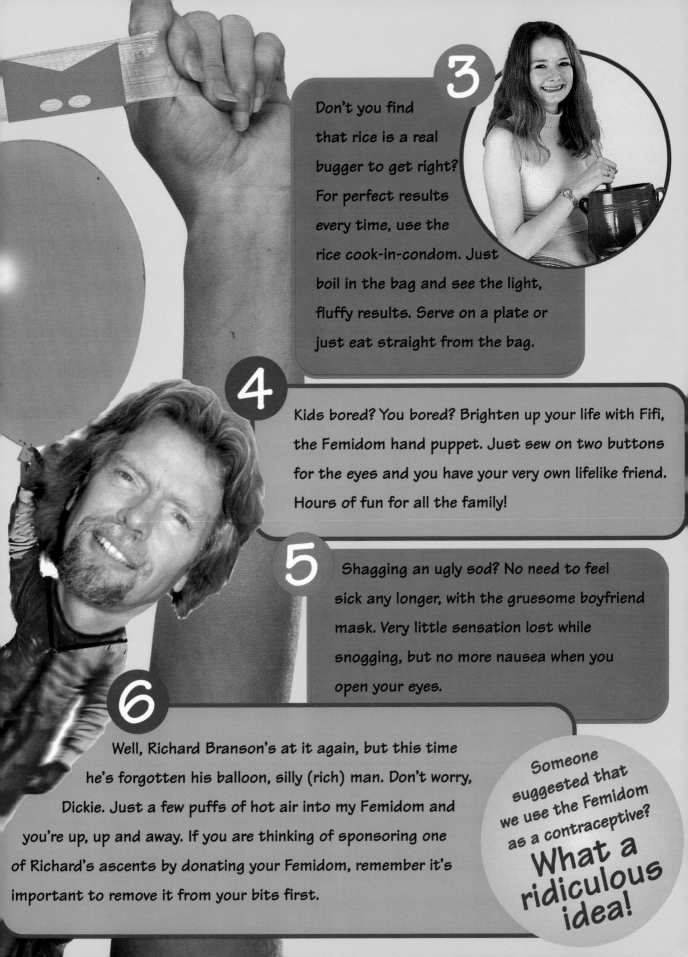

3

Don't you find that rice is a real bugger to get right? For perfect results every time, use the rice cook-in-condom. Just boil in the bag and see the light, fluffy results. Serve on a plate or just eat straight from the bag.

4

Kids bored? You bored? Brighten up your life with Fifi, the Femidom hand puppet. Just sew on two buttons for the eyes and you have your very own lifelike friend. Hours of fun for all the family!

5

Shagging an ugly sod? No need to feel sick any longer, with the gruesome boyfriend mask. Very little sensation lost while snogging, but no more nausea when you open your eyes.

6

Well, Richard Branson's at it again, but this time he's forgotten his balloon, silly (rich) man. Don't worry, Dickie. Just a few puffs of hot air into my Femidom and you're up, up and away. If you are thinking of sponsoring one of Richard's ascents by donating your Femidom, remember it's important to remove it from your bits first.

Someone suggested that we use the Femidom as a contraceptive?

What a ridiculous idea!

Losing Your Virginity

Virginity, like acne, is something most teenagers are desperate to lose. It is also similar to acne, in that both may disappear after a quick pricking with something the size of a sewing needle.

In an ideal world, we would all have our cherries popped by that most sensitive and caring of lovers – a man who truly appreciates the deeply special gift we are entrusting to him. Sadly, however, waiting for such a man is normally unfeasible. By our forties, most of us are menopausal and beginning to go off sex anyway.

The best advice, then, is just to lie back and think of England (not the whole team, of course, but Les Ferdinand and Robbie Fowler are a good start). Losing your virginity is not difficult, since men will say all manner of things to persuade us girls to have sex with them. Due to the complexity of the male psyche, most of these are very sophisticated and clever propositions, such as "please have sex with me".

Other things men may say to persuade you to have sex with them
(AND WHAT THEY REALLY MEAN)

"You would if you really loved me"
(I'M GOING TO TELL THE LADS YOU DID ANYWAY, SO WHAT HAVE YOU GOTTA LOSE?)

"I'm a very considerate lover"
(I WON'T BORE YOU AFTERWARDS BY TALKING TO YOU)

"I'm very sexually experienced"
(I SOMETIMES TUG ON THE OLD TODGER UP TO FIFTEEN TIMES A DAY)

"You'll get so much out of it"
(I WILL PAY YOU)

GUYS ARE A REAL SUCKER FOR A VIRGIN. EVEN THE BIBLE SAYS SO – ALTHOUGH IN FACT WHAT IT SHOULD HAVE SAID WAS:

"And lo, there didst come to the City of Bethlehem a virgin. And verily the Three Wise Men didst journey many weary miles to see the virgin, bringing beautiful gifts. But on arrival, they couldst not get near, thanks to the drooling horde of Moronic Desperate Men already trying to chat her up."

Taking a woman's maidenhood is seen as an indication of true masculinity, like possessing a complete set of Esso World Cup Collection coins. If he thinks you're a delicate, chaste creature of pure and unspoiled virtue – he's guaranteed to want to get inside your pants. (**Amazing But True: because of this, 90% of adult men regularly fantasise about Sister Wendy Beckett.**)

To this end, a sachet of tomato ketchup (appropriated from the restaurant when your date is in the toilet) can be punctured with a fork and carefully inserted for later on. The results are surprisingly authentic. Try this with curry sauce and you might even get him to go down on you more than once.

Let's get one thing clear before we start. EVERY woman, at one time in her life, has faked an orgasm. So if you're a man reading this and thinking, "They must have done it with other men, not me, I can tell the difference", then let me put suspicion and doubt into your mind about every woman that you thought you'd sent to heaven and back. Probably the closest place you sent her was the nearest newsagent for some chocolate.

If you are questioning this, then let me remind you ... Meg Ryan in *When Harry Met Sally*.

No doubt there are men out there somewhere doing wonderful things to very grateful women, while most of us are still staring at the ceiling thinking ...

POW!

Fakir

THE OBJECT OF FAKING

1 TO MAKE THE MAN FEEL BETTER

To me this is a pointless exercise. If he's not doing things that make you moan (and I'm not talking about doing the washing up), then

(a) if you actually like the man in question, be kind and tell him that he's way off the mark and nothing's going to happen, even if he keeps doing what he's doing till Christmas. Let him finish crying and then tell him to find the peanut butter;

(b) if you hardly know him and you're only in bed with him 'cos someone told you he had a knob larger than Linford, then why give him the satisfaction of thinking he's a sex god, when he's only the David Icke of the God world.

2 TO GET IT OVER WITH

Let's face it, women only fake to get it over with faster, and there's nothing more a man would like than to come as quickly as he likes. So let's start being honest and, instead of all that mock moaning that would probably win a BAFTA award, try phrases such as ...

"You can stop now"

"Wait while I get a Femidom"

"Remember the biscuit game"
(yes, we know all about it!)

If all else fails and you're not going to experience ecstasy until the next episode of *Home and Away*, then here's a list of a few things that you could be thinking of.

1 His best friend
2 What colour to paint the ceiling
3 The entire Welsh rugby team
4 Being smeared with a dozen melting king-size Galaxy bars
5 Your brother's best friend
6 The spin cycle on your Hotpoint.

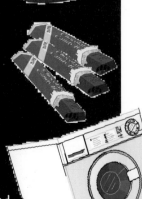

SEX

I N S T R U C T I O N

ONE THING GUARANTEED TO PUT A SMIDGEN OF STRAIN ON A RELATIONSHIP IS TELLING YOUR BLOKE

HE'S CRAP IN BED

Strange as it may seem to you it's going to come as a complete surprise to him that Serge Gainsbourg is not his natural father.

The first thing to remember is that he thinks that grabbing at your breasts like he would at two ferrets escaping from a drainpipe is a big turn on and that farting and blow jobs

when combined are somehow the peak of eroticism. So here we recommend a few ideas to help break the news gently and one or two suggestions for helping his technique:

Put a big note on the packet of condoms saying 'in, out – do not be afraid to repeat a number of times'.

Take out a full page in the local newspaper and put a picture of a bed with a dog turd in it with a foot-high caption (include name and address as appropriate) 'That's You That Is'.

Take a wooden spoon to bed and when he turns away to go to sleep, poke him in the back with it and see how he likes it.

Tell him you're going to buy him a moped for his birthday and when he asks why tell him they work on only two strokes as well.

POSITIONS

FOR HIM TO TRY

MISSIONARY POSITION

he gets on his knees in front of you
and prays you'll let him sleep with you

GOLDEN SHOWER

he showers you with pound coins
until you agree to sleep with him

DOGGY FASHION

you don't agree to sleep with
him until he sits up and begs

Fax him, via his mate's machine,
the name and address of David Mellor's
sex therapist, pointing out that if Mellor
is as ugly as him and can still pull,
it must be his technique.

Lines

So you got a bit tiddly and picked up a real plonker. As you contemplate your ravaged face in his bathroom mirror the next morning, you know you never want to see him again, but you want to get out without going into an Oprah-style debate about it. Here are some lines which guarantee he won't be calling you...

" CAN I BRING MY HUSBAND NEXT TIME? HE LIKES TO WATCH. "

" HAVE YOU HEARD THE WORD OF THE LORD? "

" I'M UP IN COURT TOMORROW FOR ASSAULTING MY EX-BOYFRIEND. "

" I MUST GO AND COLLECT THE CHILD BENEFIT FOR MY FIVE LITTLE GIRLS. "

" I BET YOU'VE NEVER HAD A PRACTISING WITCH BEFORE. "

" I'VE GOT A FEW IDEAS ON HOW YOU COULD MAKE THIS PLACE MORE HOMELY. "

" NO BREAKFAST FOR ME, HAVE YOU GOT ANY WHISKY? "

A girl's favourite names for man's best friend

(and we're not talking about his dog)

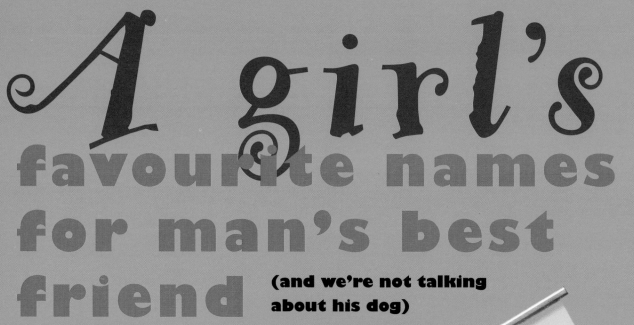

Pump-action love gun

BANG

Panty Plunger

Dingle Dangle

Willy Wonker and the white chocolate factory

Cyclops

Percy, the purple person with the pink polo neck

Tommy Todger

yum yum

Wriggly's chewing gum

Purple-helmeted
pot-holer

John Thomas
the Tank Engine

Mmmmm

Heat-seeking
moisture missile

Mr Big (only to be used
when you want something)

Phyllis
the Phallus

Sex
AND POLITICIANS

• • • • • EXCLUSIVE • • • •

Apparently, power is the ultimate aphro-disiac. Presumably this explains why Antonia de Sancha could not resist an affair with the man who was then in charge of the Lottery and listed buildings – heady stuff.

BUTT UGLY

Sex and politicians is not a new combination, dating from Lloyd George to Profumo and, of course, JFK. However, nowadays this seems to have proliferated to a full-time business. The odd thing about the affairs of latterday British politicians, however, is that the men involved have all been, with-out exception, butt ugly.

Yes, most of our politicians for some inexplicable reason are hideous – that's just the way things are. In the same way that basketball players are tall, opera singers are fat and jugglers have no friends.

This was an issue when Tony Blair became leader of the Labour Party. Many commentators said that he was chosen in part because he's a pretty boy – pretty compared to Margaret Beckett, possibly.

We all know that in the city of the blind, the one-eyed man is king, but standing him next to Robin Cook or John Gummer does not make Tony Blair attractive. (Anyway, most of us prefer his dad, Lionel.)

Nevertheless, the fact remains that these men in parliament (who, if you met them in your local, would make you puke on your shoes) do manage to get laid.

PRIME
SLEAZEBALL

DAVID MELLOR

Strange resemblance to a mutant amphibian. The gap in his teeth alone is enough to frighten off any sensible girl, although it may be popular in Somalia.

CECIL PARKINSON

A man so slimy that he was asked to account for his whereabouts at the time of the Orkneys slick. Managed to father a child by his mistress, got her to look like the villain, was taken back by his wife and made a Lord for his trouble. Nice work.

STEVEN NORRIS

This man had five mistresses on the go at once. Not a pretty boy, with more chins than Michael Jackson's had noses. However, the glamour of his position as a junior transport minister obviously turned a few heads (360 degrees in many cases, one might suspect).

ALAN CLARK

Face like a prune and the personality to match. Bragged about sleeping with a judge's wife and her daughters. Also claimed to have fancied Margaret Thatcher, something not even Denis has ever admitted to in public. Clearly as mad as a box of frogs.

JEFFREY ARCHER

Definitely not to be included in the shagging list.

JOHN MAJOR

Sadly, it is indicative of John's complete lack of charisma that when there were rumours of an affair with his caterer, he didn't even need to deny it. Nobody actually believed for a moment that our Prime Minister had shagged anybody ever.

Allegedly...

How to stop your

OK, let's face facts. If a man's alive and conscious, his eye will rove. The poor dear is genetically programmed to try to spread his seed in as many different pastures as possible. But don't despair, it's very easy to keep a man tilling only in your field. First, a few important points to remember:

1. Any girl worth her salt knows that no man's worth really chasing or getting upset about, but it's fun to play a little game and kick him into touch, just to prove you can do it. Then you can always dump him once you've flexed your muscles.

2. Girls' eyes rove just as much as boys'. We just hide it better and can act loyal and true till the cows come home and they believe us. New evolutionary research suggests that we women are in fact genetically programmed to want sperm competition between **different men's sperm** on the **inside**!

3. Even if he does stray, he'll regret it. They always do. They don't know what they want, they just think they do!

Things to DO...

1. Sock him in the eye with a cricket bat to give him a permanent lazy eye, so he's got a good excuse for its constant roving.

2. Flirt with his best friend all night whilst wearing his team's football kit. You can be sure where his eyes will be the whole time.

3. Make him wear blinkers.

4. Take him on a visit to your local STD clinic.

5. Tell him it's fine for him to have a drink with another woman, as long as he doesn't mind the fact that after you've finished with her, she'll be drinking all her solids through a straw.

Boyfriend's... ROVING EYE

Things NOT to do...

1. Cry, cling to him and sob, "Don't leave me, please don't leave me, I can't live without you."

2. Ask him to fill in daily reports detailing his every activity, place of activity, and the names and addresses of all vertebrates that he touched, spoke to, saw or thought about during his every waking and sleeping moment.

3. Assume that any of his friends called Pat, Les, Tony or Florence are necessarily girls.

4. Count his condoms hourly and have him arrested if you cannot account for any fluctuations in numbers.

A BEDTIME STORY FOR YOU TO READ TO A BOYFRIEND WITH A ROVING EYE

Once upon a time there was a Prince and Princess and they were very much in love. Then, one day, the Prince's eyes began to rove. They roved so much that the tendons behind his eyes contracted and pulled his penis back into him. Each time his eyes were roving, his penis contracted a little bit more and he was soon a very poor excuse for a Prince and crap in bed.

His eyes kept roving and started to roll right up into his head and he began to look truly gross. He lost his position as Prince, had no gold coins and had to live under a railway bridge, like a troll, collecting copper coins from people who found him entertainingly freaky, with his tiny cock and back-to-front eyes.

Finally, one day, his eyes were roving as usual, albeit only on women who had come to laugh at him and show him to their boyfriends as a warning, when suddenly the wind changed and his eyes got stuck backwards forever. He went totally blind and was hit by a train and splattered across the tracks. His tiny cock was sliced in half by a train wheel, releasing millions of tiny maggots that had been feasting inside his rotting, unused acorn.

The Princess shook her head sorrowfully for a few minutes when she heard of this tragedy and then got on with shagging the brains out of her new, hugely dicked Prince.

There are (as you go through life and relationships) certain patterns that emerge and which seem to crop up with unfailing regularity. Many women have become convinced (and there is currently scientific research being done) about the theory that men are genetically programmed with a script. You know the script. After three or four blokes have tried to get out of making even the slightest commitment with the "I need more space" line, which often translates into "I fancy your sister/ best friend/mother", you can, when one of the lines is trotted out, quite confidently join in the recital. You'll even be able to finish his sentences and pre-empt his excuses.

Thus all arguments can be distilled down to one key phrase from the script. You thought he was some wondrous and unique individual – a man with original thoughts and emotional honesty. Read on and weep.

This brings us to an important point. As a sociologist would put it, you should never shag down the scale. Some women do, in the mistaken opinion that by dating a pig they will be sorted forever after. They believe they have a partner for life and that he'll be so grateful he'll never look elsewhere. Oh, how wrong they are! The simple fact that you are dating him will immediately up his status. He will be treated with respect by men and women alike and will assume an air of undeserved mystery. "What has he got, does he do, does he pack, to pull her? He must have hidden depths."

Unaccustomed to this kind of attention, his head will swell, along with other parts of his anatomy. (If you don't believe it, just give a moment's thought to Christie Brinkley and Billy Joel. In a short space of time it went from "uptown girl" to that short, fat, singing pig, telling her she was letting herself go.) In your case, rows along the lines of "I only shagged you out of pity" will ensue and someone will get killed.

FAVOURIT
WITH YOUR

ARGUMENT TWO

"Don't crowd me."

Translation

"I need to make you feel insecure to adjust the power balance in my favour, because I find I want to spend all my time with you and my mates are taking the piss." Sometimes called the classic transference row, as you in bewilderment remind him of all the times he has turned up at your house at two in the morning on the nights you'd agreed t~~ ~~... your own thi~~...~~

ARGUMENT THREE

"Can we keep it casual? You can see other people as well."

Translation

"I managed to pull a girl as attractive and clever as you when I had a crap haircut and no dress sense. Now I've smartened up, under the influence of your taste and style, I wonder if I might be able to do even better. However, I don't want to risk losing you, so I'll dress this manipulative gambit up in a token illusion of equality."

There are some scenarios that men say are ever-familiar, insisting that women are just as predictable in their row-causing behaviour. Let us examine the evidence.

YOU SAY "You don't love me any more, you're seeing someone else."
HE SAYS "You're wrong, you are just imagining things because you are neurotic."
ANALYSIS
You are right. Always trust your suspicions. He is just stalling until a convenient moment comes along for him to walk out.

YOU SAY "Please could you put the rubbish out, it's too heavy for me and it's been there for three days."
HE SAYS "Nag, nag, nag. I never get a moment's peace from you, you old hag."
ANALYSIS
Kill him, he's dog-meat. Put his remains out with the rubbish. No-one will know – it smells already.

E ARGUMENTS

BOYFRIEND

A GIRL'S GUIDE TO THE BANGER

SAUSAGE (*sosij*, n.): Pork or other meat, seasoned, and stuffed into long cylindrical cases, prepared from entrails or other synthetic material and divided when full into lengths of a few inches by twisting or tying; (colloquial) sausage-shaped object, or derogatory – a German sausage.

Mmm Mmmm. When you put it like that, how can you resist, you German sausage!!! If you're not put off by that rather tempting description, then here's a breakdown of some of the more popular artery-hardening unknown quantities that are sausages.

The Frankfurter – origin Germany (though not strictly from Frankfurt or made by someone called Frank). Strangely, it happens to rhyme with "inserter", which the Germans would have overlooked because they speak German.

Cumberland Sausage – origin obvious. Cumberland is now known as Cleveland, where the large sausage caused a bit of a stir-fry and had to be taken into custody, accused of getting into the pan with the smaller less mature Lincolnshire Sausages, and boasting about the size of its girth.

Italian Salami – initially very tasty and attractive, but once you get beneath its tough outer skin you will find it pink and fatty, leaving a very tacky aftertaste.

Quorn – origin unknown. This is the John Wayne Bobbit of the Sausage Kingdom. Made from off cuts of odds and sods and reconstituted, Quorn is an unknown quantity. It tries to emulate other, more interesting sausages such as the already mentioned Lincolnshire, but is largely dull and uninteresting. It has a new skinless video due for release.

Posh Sausages – There's nothing more that poshies like than putting their wet salivating lips around big, plump, juicy sausages. But no tiny chipolatas for Mr Big Car (small sausage). Old big bucks doesn't want BSE leftovers jammed into his mouth, he wants to taste the minced tenderness of tenderloin, feel the fear of veal, and munch on anything that became a meal long before it had a chance to reach puberty. The press captured Camilla Parker-Bowles as she stuffed a king-size portion into her mouth, leading to the inspired quote "Camilla Porker-Bowles". From this we saw the birth of the Camilla Sausage, said to have rough old skin on the outside but plenty of stuffing inside. This inspired a list of other famous sausages...

The Stringfellow – made from young breast and prime rump and stuffed into very tight skins. Served with scrag-end trying to get into very tight skins.

The Michael Jackson – very artificial in appearance and taste, and loses its colour easily, but very popular with children.

The Oprah Winfrey – this sausage started life as quite a small sausage, then it was large, then small and then large again. Currently it's being sold as small, but the packaging is still large. A very confused sausage.

The Pamela Anderson: <u>WARNING</u> – this sausage contains 55% artificial stuffing and very little substance. Watch out for the message on the box, "Don't Call Me Pork!"

Dreamboys

FORGET FANTASY FOOTBALL.

Any girl worth her hypo-allergenic latex is constantly updating her mental shag-list, picking the perfect mix of talent and ball control. We may have real-life boyfriends (note the use of the plural here), but we can name our top dreamboys at the drop of a pair of knickers. This tasty menu (twelve courses) is who we'd like to see in our beds — not just in our heads.

♥ BRAD PITT

Ever since the ex-Levi-ad kid lit up Geena Davis's Christmas tree in the Big O scene in Thelma & Louise, we've wanted a bit of his action. With his slimline pecs, blond hair, blue eyes and cute butt, we don't care if Legends of the Fall was total baloney, Brad is sex on a stick.

♥ KEANU REEVES

Young, dumb and full of cum-to-bed naive sex-appeal, half-Hawaiian bad actor turned bad pop star Keanu is the mystical, confused surf dude we'd hate to have in our lives but love to have in our knickers. You can ride our bus anytime, big boy.

❤ THE BRUVVERS GALLAGHER

Noel (brains) and Liam (brawn) would definitely maybe feature in our dreamboy list. What is it about messing with brothers? Noel could provide the small talk, while Liam could use his "fook off" scowly lips for something altogether different. We reckon we could tame these bolshie bad boys so they'd be just wonderwall.

❤ DAMON ALBARN OR MARK OWEN

We wanna pick them up from school. We wanna wipe their noses and ruffle their floppy fringes. We wanna mother these little boy lost mothers and then shag 'em stupid.

❤ THE LADS FROM *FRIENDS*

They've got square haircuts, cool lines and dress well enough to bring home to our mums. Yup, Joey, Chandler and Ross are the kind of down-to-earth twentysomething guys we could actually get our mits on (if it wasn't for the fact they're trapped in a TV show). We don't care, we'll take 'em all (and the monkey!)

❤ THE DOCS FROM *ER*

Dr Doug, Dr Carter and Dr Greene can practise their bedside manner on us anytime. Getting ill never looked so good. These minxy medics have had us crowding hospital casualty departments, desperate for the home-grown equivalent. Doctor, Doctor, can you give us an internal?

❤ ❤ RIVER PHOENIX & KURT COBAIN (RIP)

We still fancy these blond, sensitive artistes, even though they're six feet under. After all, they say the only good guy's a dead guy, and at least these sweeties ain't gonna cheat on us.

❤ THE DIET COKE-AD LAD

If American model Lucky Vanous was a National Lottery prize, we'd be queuing for tickets every day (you couldn't help wanting to feel Lucky). We'd let this construction worker wolf-whistle us and swap shirts afterwards. Shame it's only a can he's sipping from, eh!

❤ EWAN McGREGOR

Lick those lips (his!). Pale, skinny, ruff-and-ready looking and with a Scottish accent that makes us want to toss him like a caber onto our futons. Ew's got those "just got out from under your skirt" eyes too, which are oh, so horny.

❤ THE EURO '96 SQUAD: DAVID SEAMAN, ALAN SHEARER JAMIE REDKNAPP

This was the summer that footie totty really entered our vocabulary. These spunks have got all the good moves and they can pass those balls our way anytime.

❤ PA WALTON

He's just a good ol' wholesome country boy, the Alpen cereal of the male totty world. Not only is he a rugged, caring older guy, but he's packed full of family values and spawned JohnBoy Jnr too. Now that's what we call a real man.

❤ KEN CLARKE

He's a bit of a lad, he's got potloads of power and bags of (our) money to boot — guess that comes from being the Chancellor of the Exchequer. Every girl's gotta have a bad-taste political lust object (even if it does only surface after the tenth Sea Breeze).

Dear Claire... ?

f you want to know why girls today are behaving worse, you have to look at the most important source of our Facts of Life and guide to sexual morals – the Agony Aunts in the problem pages of newspapers and magazines. Initially, before you had any life experience to judge things against, the outpourings of these out-of-touch, overpaid hacks was regarded as gospel. From the way they wrote, you would think these self-appointed monstrous Girl Guides had lived their lives in a windowless concrete box. Unfortunately, the more juvenile the publication, the more ridiculous the advice. Teen mags were the worst and committed a huge crime against young girls that cannot be rectified by the twee, "Are We Shocking You Yet?" sex-fests of our current glossy monthlies.

We all remember the useless "stop eating sweets until you're a size eight and join a club to meet other losers" standard replies. Here are some of the questions and the answers we would have got:

Dear Claire
My boyfriend says I'm too big (I'm a size 14) and he's too embarrassed to be seen out with me.

What can I do?
Depressed, (age 17)
Glasgow

Dear Claire
I think I am in love with Take That and, since they're split up, I've cried myself to sleep every night. Please help.

Alex

Dear Depressed,
Tell him three inches is too small for you and you're off to find yourself a real man.

Dear Alex,
If you are female, have patience. Once you hit puberty it will all fade away and be like a dream, and you will be free to find yourself a real man. If you are male, the fact that you enjoy their music would indicate that you are gay. There are many discos that play high-energy pop such as this, where you should go and find yourself a real man.

Dear Claire,

My best friend calls me lard-arse and I have a problem with acne. I fancy a boy in our class called Kevin, but whenever he speaks to me I blush, and he and his mates laugh about my lack of pubic hair (my best friend told them, but it's not really true).

I'm very depressed and lonely, and every night I eat chocolate, which I later throw up in my bedroom.

Will Kevin ever ask me out?

Lisa

Dear Lisa,

Firstly, all that rubbish about chocolate being better than sex is just that – rubbish. There's no substitute for a good shag, but as you're probably too young, have a go at pleasing yourself. You'll learn all about orgasms and find your clitoris, so that in a couple of years' time, when some little jerk tries to fob you off with a quick bang, you'll know he's a sexual inadequate and you can tell all his mates.

Kevin's a waste of space. Tell him to come back once his balls have dropped, but make sure you say this loudly in a busy corridor while several classes are walking past. As for your so-called best friend, persuade your older brother to take her on a date, then once he's kissed her, have him back away wiping his mouth and saying (while he's gagging), "Thanks, you've helped me to realise that I really am gay, that was horrible".

Finding yourself a

BEFORE LOCATING their whereabouts it is important to define the literal meaning of the term "Rich Bastard". The dictionary defines them as follows: RICH – *wealthy; abounding in possessions; well supplied; fertile; abounding in nutritive qualities; of food, highly seasoned or flavoured; mellow and harmonious (voice).* BASTARD – **n. & a.** *child born out of wedlock; an impure, coarse brown refuse product of sugar refining, used to colour beer; slang swearword for horrible bloke.* Therefore "Rich Bastard" means: a) *fertile child born out of wedlock;* b) *a mellow and harmonious voice used to colour beer;* c) *highly flavoured refuse product;* d) *highly seasoned child;* e) *child born out of wedlock with a mellow and harmonious voice;* f) *a wealthy horrible bloke.* Parts a) to e) are self explanatory. They are rarely found but research has shown that they do exist and are to be found in Eastern European countries and Magaluf. Part f), however, is easily found all over the world. In this volume we will concentrate on the English Rich Bastard (hereon referred to as RB).

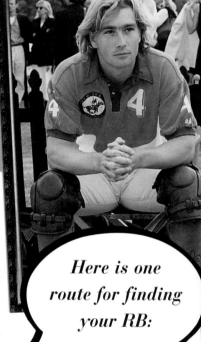

Here is one route for finding your RB:

PROJECTS TO DO

Mornings 7-8am   The Harbour Club, Chelsea.
Membership of club likely to be refused – it's very exclusive (unless you're reading this and you're name is Princess Diana). You'll have to attract the RB's attention by parking near to the club (in your hired BMW) and jumping in and out of the car at regular intervals. (Recommended time – every couple of minutes). You should be fully attired in designer exercise wear and holding exclusive holdall – bottle of mineral water an optional accessory. <u>Do not</u> under any circumstances take a close friend with ladder and camera posing as paparazzi. The club authorities will have you publicly flogged in front of club members on one of the tennis courts. (High embarrassment factor here).

Mid Morning 10-12am
Enter Stock Exchange offices disguised as a sandwich girl. Armed with Beluga caviar, fresh oysters and bottles of champagne exclaim in a deep sultry voice: " Well, it looks ~~likes~~ like your huge assets are on the rise this morning"... this should lead you easily into a literary and fruitful discussion.

RICH
BASTARD

PROJECTS TO DO

Lunchtime 1-3pm Find a packed city restaurant. Walk confidently into the middle of the room, set down your harp and with full gusto sing "If you're happy and you know it clap your hands". This will show popularity as well as your social skills. <u>NB</u> If encouraged to sing it again, try it in French.

Park car in Knightsbridge, open the bonnet, attract RB's attention by bending over into it and asking him for help with the dipstick.

Midnight Hit Stringfellows and repeat lunchtime process... once the RB becomes interested, ditch the harp— there are bigger and better G-Strings to be plucked at now.

MALE CREE

THE DJ CREEP

Chris Evans
Is this man's dick as big as his ego? Sadly for Chrissy-boy, we're not likely to try and get past the *Thunderbirds* face, dumbass jokes and enduring love affair with himself to find out.

THE VICTIM CREEP

John Wayne Bobbit
If JW thinks we're gonna give him sympathy just 'cause his wife lopped his dick off, he's got another penis extension coming. If fact, we think it's rather amusing. A top idea. Hey we may even try it ourselves. Sausages anyone?

THE SECOND-HAND CAR SALESMAN CREEP

Jeremy Beadle
Showing embarassing vidoes of ordinary folk getting hurt and humiliated again, are we? While wearing "I'm going to rip you off ma'am" big-collared suit and a bad beard. There should be a law against it.

THE POP CREEP

Michael Jackson
When male rock gods think they're Jesus Christ, kings, white women, Peter Pan, talented and interesting it's a serious recipe for serious creepdom. Give us *The Sound of Music* any day!

There's a saddo, loser, wimp, dweeb, weirdo, freaky male creep born every day — there are thousands of the blighters. The pesky vermin are everywhere and it is our job to stamp 'em out. Here's how to spot dodgy-boy types at 100 paces and take avoiding action. Set phasers to stun (on second thoughts — make that kill, with maximum drawn out agony!).

THE WORLD LEADER CREEP

Saddam Hussein

Sad Man Insane wastes all our good tabloid trivia story-space with his annoying little wars. Iraq's Mister Moustache is not only seriously unsexy, with bad clothes, but he kills members of his own family, his own people and any good jokes stone-dead. Don't date him, hate him.

THE POSH CREEP

James Hewitt

We don't like boys who grass up their girls' bed-time stories, even if they are aristo totty and the girl in question is a bonkers princess who likes watch-ing operations. Creeps lease like silicon boob-jobs, but good boys keep their mouths shut (or we'll have to get the gag out).

THE ACTION MOVIE CREEP

Arnold Schwarzenegger

Sometimes less is more. Big-action movie jerks think that if they pump themselves up into a giant penis shape, kill everything that moves and yet still have ugly faces, we'll love and respect 'em. No way, Jose. Adolescent teen boys may get off on you, but we'll shop elsewhere, ta.

THE CHAT SHOW CREEP

Richard Madeley

Don't media power couples get on your D-cups? Especially when they make shedloads of dosh and work together in such a super-cute his'n' hers fashion. Richie Rick is squeaky-clean and more cheesy than Holland. If we wanted Mummy's boy, we'd have our brothers on TV.

THE SOAP CREEP

Ian Beale from Eastenders

Wimpy, squarer than a table mat, no Mel Gibson, and really stoopid when it comes to clocking that his wife hates him! We don't care that Bealey wouldn't hurt a fly — he bugs the hell out of us! Give us that dirty old Wicksy or the Mitchell bad boys any day.

PREGNANCY
TESTING KITS

If you don't want a baby, then purchasing a pregnancy testing kit requires a great deal of courage. Just going into the chemist can turn you into a jibbering tongue-tied wreck. Beware if you choose a pharmacy where the sales assistant has a poor command of English. By the time you've repeated the words "pregnancy testing kit" several dozen times, you will probably be surrounded by hordes of giggling schoolboys, all pointing and whispering, "Cor, she's up the duff."

It is also a bad idea to try and buy a kit in a Catholic country, Rome in particular. If you can't produce a wedding ring you may be ordered out of the shop, your ears ringing with the words "puttana, puttana" (Italian for whore). If this does happen, you will be chased around the city and your bottom will be pinched until it is red raw.

TIME DELAY

Most tests take at least three minutes to work. Normally three minutes does not seem a very long time, but on this occasion it will feel like an eternity. DON'T PANIC – use this time fruitfully. Perhaps learn another language, or mend that zip you've been putting off repairing since leaving secondary school. Don't think about the consequences of the test result. It might make you very frightened indeed, and it is possible you could run away and straight into the path of an articulated lorry. You could boil an egg (or perhaps not – that might remind you of the test). Phone one of those problem message lines (most calls are a minimum of three minutes).

GUILT

Try not to blame yourself – remember you fell pregnant, that's all, and you could always explain that away by insisting that you simply fell over and had the misfortune to land on an erect penis. Look on the bright side – when you've had a baby, you can always fart in public and blame the kid. Perhaps you're expecting a boy? Just think, a penis inside you for nine months and you won't even know. Look forward to breast feeding – if you're not in a steady relationship, at least you will get to have your nipples sucked on the hour.

TEST RESULTS

Not all tests are accurate. Some expectant mothers need to do the test at least twenty-nine times before they believe the result. If you are not pregnant, breathe a sigh of relief and keep the test beside your bed at all times. It will remind you what a silly, careless little slut you were and hopefully prompt you to be more cautious in future.

Also keep a photo of the Von Trapp family beside your bed, because if you are going to have children, have as many as possible. That way they can form a close harmony singing group and make a fortune for you.

FAMOUS Slappers

Modern girls are encouraged to work hard to achieve greatness, and thankfully many do. There is, however, more than one way to skin a banana. It is high time that tributes were paid to the women who know that the way to a man's heart is not through his stomach, but actually a bit further down.

ANNA NICOLE SMITH

Playboy centrefold with huge breasts, she slapped her way to marriage with a 90-year-old oil billionaire who died about five minutes later. She wore a white wedding dress to his funeral, which was only slightly more ironic than wearing one at her wedding

BARBARA WINDSOR

Got her own back after being treated like rubbish by her dodgy first husband, by dating a succession of toy boys. Everyone assumed she would be dumped for someone younger, but she turned the tables. Currently playing "old bag" Peggy in Eastenders.

FERGIE

Slapped her way on to the front page of the tabloids with the most revolting pictures of having her toes sucked by an ugly, bald American. Helped to modernise the image of the Royal Family by showing that any girl is entitled to shag a pig, if she feels like it.

CAMILLA PARKER-BOWLES

Diana, widely acknowledged to be one of the most beautiful women in the world, must have banged her head against several walls in frustration, trying to work out how she nicked her bloke. There was a clue in the taped phone call between Camilla and Charles. He said he wished he could be her tampon and, instead of being totally grossed out and hanging up, she cooed her assent.

You see, the point is that Charlie is an old nerd and Camilla knows how to keep him happy. Also, as many men will tell you, you don't look at the mantelpiece when you are stoking the fire. So congratulations to Camilla! All the work-outs, designer clothes and eyelash tints in the world can't give you that certain sexual _je ne sais quoi._ Yes, Camilla has given hope to facially challenged women everywhere.

CYNTHIA PAYNE

Made her living as a slapper, and later as a madam who accepted Luncheon Vouchers as payment. Her no-nonsense attitude to the sex industry brought her fame and two films based on her life. A college chaplain once asked her to give a talk to his students and commented that it must be unusual to be asked for her phone number by a priest. "You'd be surprised", she replied.

MAE WEST

Set the standard for slappers everywhere. The best one-liners in the business: "It's not the men in my life, it's the life in my men", "A hard man is good to find", etc. The Dorothy Parker of sleaze. She scorned Hollywood actors in favour of labourers and cowboys, thereby avoiding the gossip columns and getting herself a damn good shag. Top woman!

MARILYN MONROE

Poor Marilyn, screen goddess, sex symbol and Hollywood slapper. Not only did she shag brothers, they were also the most important brothers in the world (after the Everly Brothers). She slapped her way to marriage with one of America's foremost writers, Arthur Miller, as well as all-American hero Joe DiMaggio. Sadly, shagging the most famous men in the world did not bring her the same comfort and happiness that can always be relied upon from a bottle of vodka and a handful of barbiturates.

Hen Nights

A woman's wedding day is quite possibly the most cherished and momentous event of her life. So it's only fair that we, your bosom girlie buddies, should try to make you feel as degraded, embarrassed, hung-over and generally cack as possible on the morning of this milestone occasion.

This is why the Hen Night was invented.

Hen Night (*n.*) **1.** *a gathering of noisy birds, sizing up any cock in the vicinity and hoping ultimately for a good lay;* **2.** *a party at which an amusing rubber chicken is produced.*

Hen Nights are subtly different from Stag Nights. On his Stag Night, a guy will frequently regain consciousness in an unfamiliar place to find himself wearing women's underwear. Conversely on her Hen Night, a girl will frequently regain consciousness in an unfamiliar place to find herself not wearing any women's underwear.

Hen Nights are a great opportunity for the blushing bride to have a thoroughly excellent piss -up and not be expected to buy any drinks. This explains why Liz Taylor is still so loaded. Whenever she's in the mood for a really good party, she just fixes a date for her next wedding.

A successful Hen Night should, like the wedding ceremony itself, be an extravagant and well-planned affair, which the bride will remember for the rest of her life (whether she wants to or not).

Donna's Hen Night

VENUE: THE OLD PORK SWORD PUBLIC HOUSE, BRISTOL
TIME: 8.30PM – 5AM

THE ENTRANCE OF THE BRIDE-TO-BE

Heralded by traditional crap Karaoke rendition of
Gloria Gaynor's "I Will Survive" by the Bride-to-Be's Best Mate, Trace.

ALL SHALL THEN STAND FOR:

THE MAKING OF THE
TRADITIONAL "WEDDING TACKLE" JOKES

During which the assembled girlie congregation shall Get A Few In,
before proceeding to the Dong Hung Lo Cantonese-style Restaurant for:

THE SLAP-UP CHINESE MEAL

Accompanied by The Ceremonial Throwing of the Rice. Those of
the congregation not completely rat-arsed shall then return to the pub for:

THE ARRIVAL OF THE STRIP-A-GRAM

All present shall giggle drunkenly for the reading of the Naff Poetic Greeting.
Music: "Get Yer Kit Off" (Trad) – arranged and sung by Bride's Mates.

THE BRIDE-TO-BE SHALL THEN KNEEL FOR:

THE REMOVAL OF THE
STRIP-A-GRAM'S UNDERGARMENTS

May be accompanied by the Performing of an
Embarrassing Simulated Sex Act in Front of Everyone.

THE KISS (WITH TONGUES)

The Best Mate shall present the Bride-to-Be with the
Ribbed Pineapple-flavoured Condom.

THE HAPPY COUPLE (BRIDE AND GORILLAGRAM)
SHALL THEN PROCEED BACK TO HER PLACE FOR:

THE SHAG AND THE EXCHANGE OF BODILY FLUIDS
AND
THE TAKING OF THE PHOTOGRAPHS

Professionally mounted and leather-bound (the Bride-to-Be – not the photos),
these will be caught on Polaroid and presented to the Newlyweds for black-
mail purposes on their return from honeymoon.

Weddings AND *Marriage and How to Avoid Them*

A regular boyfriend is a pleasant enough accessory to a busy girl's lifestyle. You stick with him because he's a good laugh and on the looks front, doesn't turn milk (or heads). He's willing in bed and has lots of money that he can't spend all by himself. Then out of nowhere he goes and spoils it all by asking you to do something truly obscene and unnatural. One minute he's going down on you, the next he's down on one knee.

CALL THE POLICE!

Long-term monogamy is for girls who think the M & S lingerie department is a bit racy.

Marriage had its uses in the days when loose women were stoned in the street — hence the myth grew up of its popularity with the female sex. As a medieval alternative to being burned at the stake for laughing, it was quite attractive. In the 1990s it's as relevant as the ducking stool.

So, if he's started to go all doe-eyed whenever he hears "Lady in Red", there are three great ways to ensure you avoid developing a husband.

1 *Be a dreadful cook and make a really bad cup of tea.*

2 *Let it be known that your family is a bit inbred. Your brother's also your uncle.*

3 *Drop things. Expensive things.*

IF ALL ELSE FAILS ... STOP CLEANING YOUR TEETH.

YOUR BEST FRIEND'S WEDDING

YOU KNOW HOW IT IS, YOU'VE BEEN BEST MATES FROM THE DAY SHE RIPPED THE HEAD OFF YOUR SINDY AND YOU FLUSHED HER "MY LITTLE PONY" DOWN THE TOILET. YOU SPENT YOUR TEEN YEARS TEACHING EACH OTHER HOW TO KISS (IF ONLY YOUDVIDEOD THAT YOU WOULD BE A PORN QUEEN MILLIONAIRE!) AND YOUR 20'S PULLING 'EM AND DUMPING 'EM IN SHORT SKIRTS AND NO KNICKERS. AND THEN **THAT DAY COMES...**

DAN ASKED ME TO MARRY HIM, LAST NIGHT!

THIS WAS BEFORE HE CAME, RIGHT?

NO, HE REALLY ASKED ME, AND I SAID YES!

BUT YOU'RE TOO PRETTY TO GET MARRIED YOU ALWAYS FANCIED HIS BROTHER, YOU CAN'T, YOU'RE MY BEST MATE!

STRATEGIES TO STOP HER FROM MARCHING DOWN THE AISLE TOWARDS 12 STONES OF OFFAL IN AN OVERTIGHT SUIT...

TELL HER YOU HAVE A LIFE THREATENING ILLNESS AND SHE CAN'T GET MARRIED 'TILL SHE'S SEEN YOU THROUGH YOUR TREATMENT.

PAY FOR A STRIPPER TO GO TO HIS STAG NIGHT AND GET COMPROMISING PICTURES TO SHOW...

...HER!

PAY FOR A MALE STRIPPER TO GO TO HIS STAG NIGHT AND GET COMPROMISING PICTURES TO SHOW...

...HER DAD!

ULTIMATE SACRIFICE. GET PISSED AND GET OFF WITH HIM. BIT DODGY THIS ONE BECAUSE SHE MIGHT JUST BUY A HANDGUN AND DRIVE YOU BOTH TO THE DOCKS!

THIS HAS FAILED. SHE WANTS YOU TO BE BRIDESMAID, AND TO WEAR PINK!

HOW DO YOU ESCAPE THIS DREADED TASK?

1. GET PREGNANT. DRASTIC, BUT IT WILL DEFINITELY WORK.

2. START SOME SERIOUS EATING. SHE WON'T WANT A PIG IN HEELS FOLLOWING HER DOWN THE AISLE. ESPECIALLY NOT A PIG IN A PINK TUTU.

3. BUY A HANDGUN AND DRIVE THEM BOTH TO THE DOCKS. THOSE CEMENT BOOTS ARE MIGHTY PERSUASIVE.

4. CHOP YOUR LEGS OFF.

THE DREADED DAY ARRIVES, YOU'RE WEARING SALMON AND YOU DON'T EVEN FANCY THE BEST MAN.

IT'S NOT TOO LATE — YOU STILL HAVE THE CEREMONY AND RECEPTION.

INVITE ALL HER EX-BOYFRIENDS, INCLUDING THE ONE SHE SAID HAD THREE LEGS.

INVITE ALL HIS EX-GIRLFRIENDS, AND IF YOU CAN DIG OUT AN ILLEGITIMATE CHILD.

INVITE AN EXTREME **RELIGIOUS** OR POLITICAL **TERRORIST** ORGANISATION TO **BOMB THE CHURCH**

GET DRUNK, SNOG HER DAD, **GIGGLE** THROUGH THE SPEECHES, AND THEN TELL EVERYONE HOW YOU BOTH USED TO GET **SHIT-FACED** BEFORE GOING OUT ON A SATURDAY NIGHT TO PLAY "WHO CAN **PULL A PIG**", WHICH INCIDENTALLY IS HOW EVERYONE COMES TO BE GATHERED HERE TODAY.

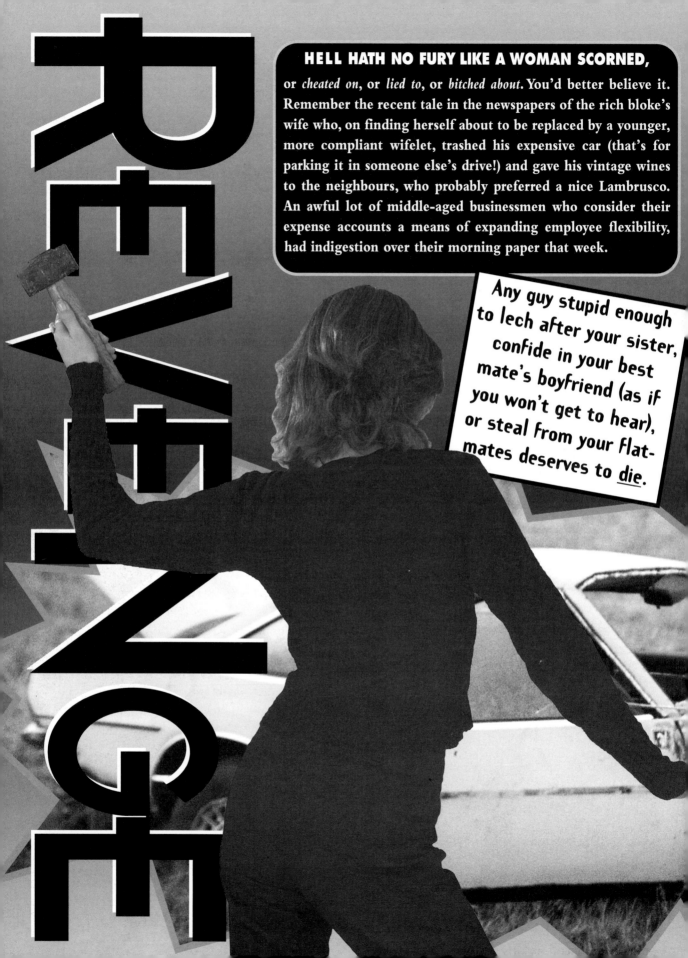

REVENGE

HELL HATH NO FURY LIKE A WOMAN SCORNED,
or *cheated on*, or *lied to*, or *bitched about*. You'd better believe it. Remember the recent tale in the newspapers of the rich bloke's wife who, on finding herself about to be replaced by a younger, more compliant wifelet, trashed his expensive car (that's for parking it in someone else's drive!) and gave his vintage wines to the neighbours, who probably preferred a nice Lambrusco. An awful lot of middle-aged businessmen who consider their expense accounts a means of expanding employee flexibility, had indigestion over their morning paper that week.

Any guy stupid enough to lech after your sister, confide in your best mate's boyfriend (as if you won't get to hear), or steal from your flat-mates deserves to <u>die</u>.

B O Y F R I E N D S

Boyfriends lie, steal or cheat. However, this should not be tolerated, not by any girl who can lie, steal and cheat quite well enough for two, thank you very much! The rule that, really inspires extra venom when broken, is the "not on your own doorstep" commandment. (Moses left that one up on Mount Sinai because two tablets were quite heavy enough, divine intervention notwithstanding, but he sure as hell told all his mates, along with commandment number thirteen ("thou shalt not ask her if she's having her period in reply to being invited in for coffee").

There is a 'truth' that women are not violent, that when it comes to the *crime passionnel* it is usually men who snap necks. The reality is that we are more devious, and our "crimes" rarely make the papers.

THE SLOW WAY

"Go on, dear, have another fried egg. I did it just the way you like it ... The doctor said it was only a little heart attack."

ne enjoyable and effective form of revenge is very simple. It requires a little ...anning or a co-conspirator. Arrange to have yourself and your betrayer, and ...baseball bat, locked inside a small, darkened room. You have hold of the ...aseball bat. Indulge yourself. A nice touch is to punctuate your speech with ...t movement, building to a crescendo.

...Okay" (nudge) *"how many times"* (tap) *"did you shag her?"* (swipe).

...Only once."

...Wrong answer" (thwack).

...on appetit!

THE QUICK WAY

"Would you be a darling and take a look at the wiring? Don't worry, I'll hold the step-ladder, it's just a bit wobbly."

UNFORTUNATELY, due to the ridiculous laws in Britain, it is often difficult to obtain the tools of the trade, such as cattle-prods and knuckle-dusters. That's when psychological torture is necessitated. An organisation called the **Female Underground Grapevine**, which stretches all over the country but is completely inaccessible to men, is the only tool needed. If a man has offended in some small or large way, been sexually indiscreet or committed a faux-pas of condom etiquette ("I'm sorry, I swear I never noticed it had slipped off"), then word of mouth will be started. It's a bit like an urban myth. Suddenly, every girl in the country will know all about his horribly deformed genitalia (untrue, of course). In every pub, club and singles bar (to which he will soon have to resort) his attempts at a chat-up line will be met with everything from open derision to pity. But never a shag. He will never know why. He will die lonely and childless, unless he has the sense to move somewhere really distant, like Peru.

After all, there's nothing noble about going to prison. Revenge is just as satisfying if no-one ever knows — in fact, more so. How pleasant to weep at the open grave, being comforted as the premature widow, when only *you* know that underneath your modest black suit you're wearing the same scarlet undies you wore to "ride" him to death. Tragic.

If all else fails, get others to do your dirty work for you. It need not be expensive; with a little imagination and a few lies, public servants can be made to work just for you.

Before you split up, did he have a bit of cash in hand? Don't keep it to yourself. The DHSS would love to know — in fact, they have a special phone line for details.

He never drank, but just before he dumped you, he had a party and one of his dodgy mates complained that he lost his "stash" somewhere in the flat. Call the police — it will still be there, as men never clean behind the sofa. How ironic that a man who treated his body like a temple should get done for Class "A".

KEEP YOURSELF AMUSED BY RINGING *CRIMEWATCH* **AND GIVING HIS NAME AS A SUSPECT. EVERY WEEK. HE'LL GET BANGED UP EVENTUALLY FOR SOMETHING HE DIDN'T DO, AND THE APPEAL WILL TAKE YEARS.**

THE Seven Ages of

Teenage Years

A huge shock for a young girl. You see, up until now you had no real awareness of gender difference. Then you hit thirteen and realise that there are people around you who dress slightly differently and are not quite as bright as you. Then you hit fifteen and they start actually talking to you. You don't know why, and you find that nothing they say is of any interest. But at the same time, you have started to change. The nausea, depression and spots that have occurred for the past two years have now manifested themselves as menstruation. You can't explain what your feelings actually mean, but you know that these dull, alien creatures who have shaky voices and bugger-all to talk about are very important to you. You then spend the next three years behaving in any way necessary to accommodate these appalling creatures just so that they will clumsily grope your tits. Rejection by spotty morons can lead to eating disorders and feelings of worthlessness, which prepare you for the next stage of female development.

Your Twenties

This is the most serious age, in terms of your ability to ruin the rest of your life completely. Every judgement you make about yourself will be intrinsically linked with boys. There will be occasions when you bring a pig home to your house for sex and, while the kettle is boiling for coffee, you rush into your bedroom to tidy it up. This is because you feel so inadequate that you actually imagine that any ugly man to whom you are offering free, uncomplicated sex would actually go into your bedroom and find magazines and knickers on the floor so disgusting that he would tell you that he has lost his hard-on and has to go home now.

Woman

Your Thirties

By this time you have seen it, done it and worn the Lycra skirt. You are wise to the guys. This is the time in a girl's life when, if she has avoided the marriage and baby trap, she has really come into her own. You know that a man's desire for a shag knows no bounds and, to facilitate that, you can have basically whatever you want. So in effect the thirties are the time for financial consolidation and humiliation. In other words, make them pay and make them pay.

Your Forties

Sexual peak time. So you've spent your thirties taking revenge for your twenties and now you achieve your peak of power. As the fount of all wisdom and sexuality, you can now pluck men like grapes. As for sex, you want the young ones and, boy do they want you. Every generation of men for the last thirty years has fantasised over Anne Bancroft in *The Graduate*. There is nothing a boy wants more than to get off with his mother's best friend. So all you need to do is hang out at school and make friends with as many mothers of young boys as possible.

Your Fifties

Disaster. Just when you have finally fathomed the mysteries of the universe, nature sends you bonkers. This is the time known as the change of life, when your hormones go berserk. It makes PMT seem like a much-missed hiatus of tranquillity. For girls who have behaved badly and remained single, you will have the blessed relief of not having to deal with men during this time of crisis, so you can be weepy or psychotic to your heart's content. Those who did get trapped, however, needn't fear too much, as the fifties are the age when husbands disappear. Always, without exception, to shag a younger woman.

Seventies/Eighties

Your working life and the majority of your dealings with men will be over, unless you are still married. Even if you are, you have to be ruthless, because your seventies should be ME time, as in *me, myself and I*. This is particularly important for those who have been wives and mothers. Now you can devote your time to art, beauty, culture and creativity. Most importantly, rheumatism and arthritis are very good excuses for smoking dope. Statistically speaking, you are likely to be on your own, as your major reward in life is to live longer than men. Now you can behave as badly as you like. It's always a good idea to pretend to be completely mad. You can push in at bus stops, and be generally rude to everybody and get away with it; and don't forget always to mention your age at every available opportunity. If you are going to manage to live that long, you might as well let everyone know about it.

Your Sixties

Now you have totally fulfilled your biological function and regained your sanity. In the past this was the time when women shrivelled up and died. No longer. Women in their sixties can now be Joan Collins. Yes, it's time to be fabulous and sexy, with no procreational implications.

OLD.E

gir

Behaving

LIZ TAYLOR

Life with Dick

So we're all going to get old one day, possibly get married, have kids and grandkids. But does that mean we start acting our age? We must party till we drop down dead. If anyone disapproves we just plead senility or Alzheimer's disease.

Let's take Elizabeth Taylor. The woman has her own suite at the Betty Ford clinic. Not only does she check herself in for a quiet rest period and detox, she also uses the facilities as a dating agency — to find and marry some sleazy bloke off a building site with a drink and drugs problem. The fact that he is some twenty years her junior means nothing. She's in her sixties and has been married eight times. At each wedding dear old Liz swears it's for life, which it would be if she was a cat and not an ageing Hollywood starlet. She claims still to be searching for the grand passion. Wise up, Liz, you should be searching for your grandchildren.

Old women feel it is their God-given right to behave badly, particularly at jumble sales or on the bus.

✈*❋❀✉ Holidays ✳❤❄☆

Kids can really get you down and most mums aren't alone in grieving for their carefree, non-dependent days. But it is still deemed very bad behaviour and highly irresponsible to forget that you have children and go on holiday to Spain leaving them at home alone. No amount of cheerful postcards or straw donkeys will make up for it.

Try and re-create that holiday atmosphere in the safety of your own home. Turn up the central heating and play the "*Gypsy Kings*" at top volume. Squeeze into your bikini, then pour yourself enough tequila to kill an elephant. When you're totally paralytic, open the window and shout at passing blokes to come in. Ask them to rub suntan oil on your back, then shag them senseless. Throw up all over them and don't give them your real phone number. Once they are gone, do a quick tidy round and bake some cookies ready for the kids when they get back from school. Don't tell your husband about your holiday – it will only ruin your marriage. *Bon Voyage*.

THE MENOPAUSE:
SIDE-EFFECTS

There are several reported cases of seemingly happily married women reaching the menopause, then going on holiday with a close woman friend somewhere exotic like Kenya. Then, instead of coming home sporting a nice tan and an assortment of hand-carved wooden animals, they stay there, divorce their husband and marry a Masai warrior. This is very, very bad behaviour. They desert their partners, children and grandchildren, all in the name of great sex. The fact that this is a country where compulsory "Clitoridectomies" are meted out with jagged rocks and primitive pickaxes seems to have slipped their minds.

The more extrovert tend to bring their warriors back home and move them into a two-up two-down council terrace in Sheffield. They ignore the looks and stares they receive from former friends and neighbours, and assume everyone is just jealous.

Unsavoury Relationships

Of course we must be cautious when we reach middle age. This is a time when some women who have been closeted all their lives can go right off the rails. They may develop very unsavoury relationships with totally unsuitable men. Take the silly old birds who think it's a good idea to become penpals with mass murderers. They write long and loving letters to serial killers and eventually marry them in the prison chapel. *This is crazy!* Here's some bloke in jail for killing his wife, several mistresses and a dozen girls he didn't even know, and there's some silly woman sitting at home thinking, "Hey now, there's the man for me. Now I've been out with some real bastards in my time, who stood me up, ripped me off, been unfaithful, but this guy's different, he's steady, he's consistent and I know where he lives".

TOY BOYS

OF COURSE when you're more mature you can enjoy the luxury of a toy boy. The Oxford definition of toy is "a thing meant rather for amusement than for serious use". If we've got lucky, married well and become a rich widow, we needn't bother with bowls or bingo for recreation. No, we can afford to employ young hunky escorts, who are paid handsomely to pleasure us. However, if you can't afford to pay for it, never mind. These days a lot of young men prefer experienced old biddies, especially if you've got dentures and don't mind removing them for added oral pleasure.

First published in 1996 by
ORION MEDIA
an imprint of Orion Books Ltd
Orion House
5 Upper St Martin's Lane
London WC2H 9EA

DESIGNED AND PRODUCED BY THE BRIDGEWATER BOOK COMPANY
Art director: Terry Jeavons **Designers:** Sara Nunan, John Christopher & Ginny Zeal

A CIP catalogue record for this book is available from the British Library

ISBN 0 75280 777 3

Repro by Pixel Colour Ltd, London

Printed and bound by Butler & Tanner Ltd, Frome and London

Picture Acknowledgements
Front cover: Rex Features Ltd. **Title page:** Rex Features Ltd. **Disgusting Things Men Do:**
(right) London Features International. **Dream Boys:** (top) Capital Features; (bottom) London
Features International. **Famous Slappers:** Capital Pictures. **Sex and Politicians:** Capital
Pictures. **Magazines:** (middle) Capital Pictures; (right/left) Rex Features Ltd. **Finding
Yourself a Rich Bastard:** Rex Features Ltd. **Girls' Night Out:** (top) London Features
International. **In/Out People:** London Features International. **Girls' Great Lessons in Bad
Behaviour:** The Bridgeman Art Library. **Girls We Love to Hate:** (right) London Features
International; (left) All Action. **Girls on Holiday:** (bottom right) London Features
International. **Heroines:** Rex Features Ltd. **Girls With Attitude:** Rex Features Ltd.
The Best Line Uttered in Any Soap: London Features International. **Girls' Films:** Katz
Pictures. **Faking Orgasms:** Kobal Collection. **Sex Instructions:** (bottom right) London
Features International. **Health & Fitness:** (left) Rex Features Ltd. **Hen Nights:** (left)
London Features International. **Blind Dates:** (right) London Features International.
The Perfect Man: London Features International. **Older Girls Behaving Badly:** London Features
International. **A Girl's Favourite Names For Man's Best Friend:** (middle) Rex Features Ltd.
Pregnancy Testing Kits: (right) London Features International. **The Female Condom:** (middle)
Capital Pictures. **The Seven Ages of Women:** (right) All Action Pictures; (left) Rex Features
Ltd. **Girls and Shopping:** All Action Pictures. **Illustrators:** Ivan Hissey, Paul Allen and
Paul Collicut.